Mastering iPadOS 26: The Ultimate User Guide to Apple's Most Powerful iPad Experience

Explore New Features, Boost Productivity, and Unlock Your iPad's Full Potential with iPadOS 26

All rights reserved. No part of this publication may be reproduced, distributed, or transmitted in any form or by any means, including photocopying, recording, or other electronic or mechanical methods, without the prior written permission of the publisher, except in the case of brief quotations embodied in critical reviews and certain other noncommercial uses permitted by copyright law.

© Finn Lautenberg, 2025

Table of Contents

Introduction **6**
    What's New in iPadOS 26 7
    Who This Guide Is For 10
    Device Compatibility and Requirements 12

Chapter 1: Getting Started with iPadOS 26 .... **15**
    Installing and Updating to iPadOS 26 15
    Navigating the New Interface 17
    Setting Up for the First Time 20

Chapter 2: Exploring the Liquid Glass Design **23**
    Understanding the New Look and Feel 23
    Customizing the Home Screen and App Icons 25
    Control Center and Lock Screen Upgrades 28

Chapter 3: The All-New Windowing System **32**
    Multitasking Reinvented: Window Resizing, Tiling & Exposé 32
    Using Stage Manager and External Displays 35
    Mastering the New Menu Bar 38

Chapter 4: Apple Intelligence Explained **42**
    What Is Apple Intelligence? 42
    Using Live Translation in FaceTime, Phone & Messages 44
    Creating with Genmoji and Image Playground 47
    Smarter Shortcuts with AI-Powered Actions 50

Chapter 5: Power Productivity Tools **54**
    New Features in the Files App 54
    Folder Customization and Dock Integration 56

Setting Default Apps for File Types........................ 58
Chapter 6: Mastering the Preview App..................... 62
Viewing and Editing PDFs and Images.................. 62
Using Markup with Apple Pencil............................. 64
AutoFill and Creating Quick Sketches.................... 67
Chapter 7: Audio, Video, and Creative Workflows.. 70
Background Tasks for Pro Users............................ 70
New Audio Input Options and Voice Isolation......... 73
Using Local Capture for High-Quality Recordings.. 77
Chapter 8: Communication Upgraded............... 83
Using the New Phone App on iPad........................ 83
A Seamless Cross-Device Experience............ 83
Setting It Up.. 84
Hold Assist and Call Screening.............................. 85
Messages Overhaul: Backgrounds, Polls & Apple Cash... 86
FaceTime Enhancements and Call Features..........89
Chapter 9: Journaling, Gaming, and Daily Life.. 93
Using the Journal App for Wellness and Reflection 93
Exploring the New Apple Games App and Game Overlay.. 98
Integrating Journal with Maps, Audio, and Media. 102
Chapter 10: Math, Notes, and Calligraphy........ 106
Math Notes and 3D Graphing in Calculator.......... 106
Using Markdown in Notes..................................... 110
Writing with the Reed Pen in Apple Pencil Apps...115
Chapter 11: Accessibility and Inclusivity.......... 120
Accessibility Reader and Braille Access............... 120
Sharing Accessibility Settings Across Devices..... 125

Customizing iPadOS 26 for Every User................128

■ **Chapter 12: Tips, Tricks & Hidden Features.....132**

Lesser-Known Features That Will Boost Your Workflow... 132

Power User Tips for Faster Navigation.................. 135

Custom Shortcuts and Automation Ideas............. 139

■ **Chapter 13: Troubleshooting and FAQs........... 143**

Common Issues After Updating............................143

Managing Storage and Performance....................148

Resetting, Restoring, and Recovery Mode........... 151

■ **Appendix..156**

Supported Devices and Feature Availability......... 156

   iPad Models Compatible with iPadOS 26....... 156

   Apple Intelligence: M-Series and A17 Pro Only.... 157

   Feature Availability Matrix...............................158

   Performance Tips for Older Devices............... 159

Apple Intelligence Language Support Timeline.... 160

   Languages Supported at Launch.....................161

   Languages Coming by End of 2025................ 162

   How to Know If a Feature Is Supported.......... 163

Additional Resources and Apple Support............. 164

   1. Apple's Official Help Resources...................164

   2. YouTube and Third-Party Tutorials............. 165

   3. Third-Party Tools and Apps........................166

   4. Accessibility Support...................................166

   5. Feedback and Reporting Bugs................... 167

Introduction

Welcome to Mastering iPadOS 26: The Ultimate User Guide to Apple's Most Powerful iPad Experience. This comprehensive guide is designed to help users of all levels explore, understand, and take full advantage of the revolutionary new features introduced in iPadOS 26. Whether you're a creative professional, an educator, a student, or simply an iPad enthusiast, this book is crafted to walk you through every significant improvement, hidden gem, and user-enhancing update packed into this landmark release.

Since its inception, iPadOS has continually evolved to bridge the gap between the portability of an iPhone and the performance power of a Mac. With iPadOS 26, Apple has made its boldest leap yet. Combining a redesigned interface, pro-grade multitasking, smarter AI, and powerful apps, this operating system transforms the iPad into a dynamic productivity and creativity powerhouse.

This guide begins with an in-depth introduction to what's new in iPadOS 26, who the update is designed for, and how to ensure your device is compatible. From there, each chapter builds upon key features and usage techniques that will enrich your everyday workflow or help you harness new creative potentials.

Let's dive into the very heart of the update and explore why iPadOS 26 is being hailed as Apple's most ambitious iPad software update ever.

What's New in iPadOS 26

iPadOS 26 isn't just a routine software update; it's a transformational shift in how the iPad functions, looks, and integrates with Apple's ecosystem. Below is an overview of some of the most groundbreaking and essential additions:

1. Liquid Glass Design A fresh new look for iPad comes with the introduction of Liquid Glass — a translucent, responsive interface layer that adapts to touch, light, and environmental changes. This design redefines aesthetics on the iPad with dynamic elements that bring greater focus and visual appeal. Home Screens, app icons, Lock Screens, and the Control Center feel more interactive, customizable, and alive.

2. Powerful and Intuitive Windowing System iPadOS 26 makes multitasking dramatically easier and more powerful. Users can now:

Resize and tile windows with fluid gestures

Save window positions for later

Use Exposé to view all open windows

Utilize external monitors more effectively

Access a universal menu bar with app-specific tools

3. Deep Integration of Apple Intelligence Apple's advanced on-device AI engine now powers multiple new features:

Live Translation in Messages, Phone, and FaceTime

Genmoji and Image Playground tools for creative expression

Smart Shortcuts that summarize, generate content, and automate tasks

4. Supercharged Files App A complete overhaul of the Files app includes:

Collapsible folders and resizable columns in List view

Folder customization with colors and emojis

Quick access via folder Dock placement

Default app settings per file type

5. Preview App Debuts on iPad Previously exclusive to macOS, Preview now comes to iPad:

View and annotate PDFs and images

Use Apple Pencil for sketching or markup

Fill out forms using AutoFill

6. Advanced Audio and Video Features

Background Tasks run powerful processes like rendering or exporting

Audio input selection per app and website

Voice Isolation and Local Capture for pro-quality recording

7. Journal and Apple Games App

Journal brings reflective writing, maps, audio, and media entry support

Apple Games app centralizes events, settings, and multiplayer features

8. Accessibility & Pen Enhancements

Reed pen with stroke-angle calligraphy for Apple Pencil

Accessibility Reader and Braille Access upgrades

iPadOS 26 reimagines how we use iPads, blurring the lines between tablet and desktop computing. It represents a future-forward leap that makes iPads more relevant than ever in both personal and professional contexts.

Who This Guide Is For

This guide is written for a diverse range of users, from everyday iPad owners looking to get more from their devices to power users and professionals pushing the iPad to its limits. Here are the primary audiences:

1. Everyday Users If you use your iPad for browsing, watching videos, messaging, or casual productivity, this guide will help you discover features like easier app switching, new customization options, and AI tools that simplify your daily tasks.

2. Creative Professionals Designers, illustrators, video editors, musicians, and digital artists will benefit from features like Local Capture, Apple Pencil enhancements, new background processing, and the debut of Preview. These tools offer faster workflows and more intuitive creative freedom.

3. Business Users & Entrepreneurs This guide will help professionals leverage iPadOS 26 to optimize multitasking, file management, and audio/video communication. Tools like Shortcuts, Files improvements, and external display support can transform your iPad into a true productivity hub.

4. Educators and Students With intelligent translation, enhanced Notes, Math Notes, 3D graphing, and journaling tools, students and teachers can streamline studying and lesson planning. AI-assisted features also support accessibility and learning diversity.

5. Accessibility Users For users with vision, motor, or reading challenges, this guide explains how iPadOS 26's new accessibility options can make interaction easier and more personalized.

Whether you're tech-savvy or just getting started, this guide will walk you through each feature clearly, step-by-step, ensuring you harness the full potential of your iPad.

Device Compatibility and Requirements

Before diving into the full experience of iPadOS 26, it's essential to understand if your device supports the new features. Apple has been strategic in balancing innovation with device longevity, but some features require newer hardware or chips.

Compatible Devices for iPadOS 26

iPadOS 26 is available as a free software update for the following models:

iPad Pro (M4, 12.9-inch 3rd-gen and later; 11-inch 1st-gen and later)

iPad Air (M2 and later; 3rd-gen and later)

iPad (A16, 8th-gen and later)

iPad mini (5th-gen and later; A17 Pro)

Apple Intelligence Requirements

Some of the most advanced features require:

Apple Silicon (M1 or newer)

Language set to a supported Apple Intelligence language (English, French, German, Italian, Brazilian Portuguese, Spanish, Japanese, Korean, Simplified Chinese)

These features include:

Live Translation

Genmoji and Image Playground

Smart Shortcuts

More languages will be added by the end of the year: Dutch, Norwegian, Swedish, Turkish, Vietnamese, Traditional Chinese, and more.

Storage and Space

Recommended storage: At least 8GB of free space before update

For best performance: Devices with 4GB RAM or more

Updating to iPadOS 26

To update:

1. Go to Settings > General > Software Update

2. Ensure your iPad is connected to Wi-Fi and has at least 50% battery

3. Tap Download and Install

If you're part of the Apple Developer Program or Beta Software Program, you may already have early access to iPadOS 26. Public release is scheduled for Fall 2025.

Understanding your device's compatibility helps ensure that you experience all the new features iPadOS 26 has to offer. Now that we've set the foundation, the next chapters will guide you through configuring and using each of these features in-depth.

Chapter 1: Getting Started with iPadOS 26

Installing and Updating to iPadOS 26

Installing iPadOS 26 is the first step in unlocking the new wave of features and design changes Apple has introduced. This chapter section will walk you through all the necessary preparations, options, and troubleshooting strategies to make your upgrade seamless and stress-free.

1. Preparing Your Device Before updating, it's essential to prepare your iPad to ensure a smooth transition:

- **Back Up Your Data:** Use iCloud or a Mac to back up your device. Go to **Settings > [Your Name] > iCloud > iCloud Backup** and tap **Back Up Now**. If using a Mac, connect your iPad via USB and use Finder to create a manual backup.
- **Free Up Space:** Ensure at least 8GB of free space to prevent interruptions. Delete unused apps or move media to cloud storage.
- **Charge Your iPad:** Make sure your iPad has at least 50% battery or is connected to power during the update.

2. Downloading the Update Once your device is ready:

- Navigate to **Settings > General > Software Update**.
- iPadOS 26 will appear if your device is compatible. Tap **Download and Install**.
- Agree to Apple's terms and wait for the download to complete.
- Your iPad will restart to install the update.

3. Alternative: Updating Through a Mac or PC
For users with connection issues or who prefer a wired update:

- Connect your iPad to your Mac and open **Finder** (or **iTunes** on Windows).
- Select your iPad, then click **Check for Update > Download and Update**.
- Enter your passcode if prompted.

4. Using the Apple Beta Software Program If you want early access to future iPadOS updates:

- Enroll your device at **beta.apple.com**.
- Download the beta profile.
- Follow the on-screen instructions to install the beta version of iPadOS 26.

5. Troubleshooting Installation Issues

- If the download is slow or stuck, ensure a strong Wi-Fi connection.
- Restart your device and try again.
- If the update fails, try using a computer or reset network settings under **Settings > General > Transfer or Reset iPad > Reset Network Settings**.

Updating to iPadOS 26 opens up a more powerful, visually rich, and intelligent experience on your iPad. With careful preparation, installation is easy and rewarding.

Navigating the New Interface

With iPadOS 26, Apple introduces a visually stunning and more dynamic user interface, centered around the new **Liquid Glass** design. This section covers how to find your way around the updated iPad experience.

1. Home Screen and App Library

The Home Screen has been reimagined:

- **Liquid Glass Aesthetic:** App icons shimmer, glow, and respond to ambient lighting.
- **Customizations:** Long-press anywhere on the Home Screen to add widgets, rearrange apps, or apply light, dark, or clear icon themes.

- **App Library:** Swipe left from your last Home Screen to access categorized app folders.

2. Lock Screen and Control Center

- **Lock Screen:** Now supports dynamic notifications and animated backgrounds. Press and hold on the clock to change widgets or wallpapers.
- **Control Center:** Redesigned with translucent elements and more customization. Access it by swiping down from the top-right corner.

3. Dock and Folder Integration

- The **Dock** remains persistent across apps and multitasking views. Now, you can drag folders from the Files app directly into the Dock for quick access.
- Custom icons and emojis can be used to make folders more recognizable.

4. App Switching and Exposé

- **Swipe Up and Hold** to view open apps.
- Tap **Exposé** (appears automatically when multiple windows are open) to see all app windows.
- Use **four or five-finger swipes** for navigation.

5. The New Menu Bar

- Appears when you swipe down from the top of the screen or hover your cursor.
- Contains app-specific options, searchable commands, and tips.
- Especially useful in multitasking and external display setups.

6. Notification Center and Widgets

- Swipe from the top-left to open the Notification Center.
- Add widgets here or to the Home Screen for quick information access.

7. Enhanced Accessibility Navigation

- Systemwide **Accessibility Reader** for simplified, readable views.
- **Braille Access Mode** adds seamless support for braille devices.

Navigating iPadOS 26 is a fluid, enjoyable experience designed with both power users and casual users in mind. Take time to explore the gestures, shortcuts, and customizable elements that give you control over your device like never before.

Setting Up for the First Time

Whether you're using an iPad for the first time or upgrading to iPadOS 26 on a new device, the setup process has never been more intuitive or customizable.

1. Initial Power-On and Setup Wizard

- Hold down the **Top button** until the Apple logo appears.
- Select your **language** and **region**.
- Connect to Wi-Fi and sign in with your **Apple ID**.
- If restoring from an old device, choose **Restore from iCloud Backup** or **Transfer Directly from iPad/iPhone**.

2. Face ID or Touch ID Configuration

- If supported, you'll be prompted to set up **Face ID** or **Touch ID** for security.
- You can skip this step and return to it later in **Settings > Face ID & Passcode**.

3. Setting Up Siri and Apple Intelligence

- Enable **Siri** and select language settings to match supported Apple Intelligence features.
- Choose whether to allow Siri to respond when locked.

4. Enable Key Services

- **Find My iPad**: Helps locate your device if lost.
- **Screen Time**: Monitor and manage app usage.
- **iCloud Services**: Choose what you want to sync across devices (Photos, Notes, Safari, etc).

5. Personalizing Your iPad

After the basic setup:

- Choose a wallpaper, Home Screen layout, and control which widgets to show.
- Visit **Settings > Display & Brightness** to toggle between light, dark, and automatic themes.
- Enable **True Tone** and **Night Shift** for optimal viewing comfort.

6. Recommended Settings After Setup

- **Software Update**: Double-check that iPadOS 26 is fully installed.
- **Privacy Settings**: Go to **Settings > Privacy & Security** to review which apps can access location, camera, and microphone.
- **App Downloads**: Visit the App Store to re-download your favorite or previously used apps.

7. Optional but Useful Settings

- **Tap to Wake**: Quickly turn on your screen with a simple tap.

- **Raise to Wake**: Enable under **Display settings**.
- **Apple Pencil Pairing**: Attach your Pencil to the side of your iPad to pair.

8. Accessibility Configuration

During or after setup, go to **Settings > Accessibility** to enable features like VoiceOver, Zoom, Magnifier, and Hearing Devices.

Setting up iPadOS 26 is a simple process that introduces you to the major enhancements right away. Customization options make it feel like your own, while intuitive steps ensure even new users get off to a confident start.

Now that your iPad is updated, explored, and customized, you're ready to take on the rich features detailed in upcoming chapters—from AI integrations to pro-level multitasking and creativity tools.

Chapter 2: Exploring the Liquid Glass Design

Understanding the New Look and Feel

iPadOS 26 introduces a dramatic visual evolution in Apple's user interface, centered around the **Liquid Glass design**—a modern, fluid aesthetic that elevates how users perceive and interact with their iPad. This chapter unpacks the innovation behind the design, its effect on usability, and how it reshapes the iPad experience across different applications.

1. What is Liquid Glass?

Liquid Glass is Apple's new UI material that creates a sense of depth, clarity, and interactivity. Unlike traditional flat or static backgrounds, Liquid Glass responds in real-time to light, motion, and user interaction. It subtly reflects surroundings and refracts colors, making each user experience feel personal and dynamic.

2. Why Liquid Glass Matters

- **Sensory Richness:** Liquid Glass brings vitality to every UI element. Whether it's the shimmer on the Lock Screen or the translucent blur

behind app windows, this design invites users to explore.
- **Contextual Awareness:** It helps focus the user's attention by adjusting visual intensity based on user input. For example, background elements blur or dim when focusing on a task.
- **Consistency Across Apps:** From Safari to Messages, Liquid Glass offers a coherent and immersive look that stretches across native and third-party apps.

3. Dynamic Responsiveness

Liquid Glass changes based on:

- **Touch input** – Tap, swipe, or hold and the background reacts fluidly.
- **Device orientation** – Rotating the iPad changes light reflection angles.
- **Theme (light or dark)** – Tints shift in brightness, saturation, and mood.

4. Accessibility Meets Design

Apple ensures Liquid Glass isn't just pretty but practical. Users with vision sensitivities can adjust contrast, reduce motion, or disable transparency under **Settings > Accessibility**.

5. Where You See Liquid Glass

- **Lock Screen**

- **Control Center**
- **Notification Center**
- **App Switcher & Dock**
- **System menus and background overlays**

Understanding the Liquid Glass design means appreciating how Apple integrates aesthetics with function. It's not merely eye candy—it's a fluid, contextual, and interactive layer that enhances every moment spent on your iPad.

Customizing the Home Screen and App Icons

Customization has always been a strong point for iPad users, but iPadOS 26 takes it a step further. With the Liquid Glass foundation in place, users now have more control than ever to make the Home Screen their own. This section explores the extensive personalization tools introduced in this update.

1. Icon Customization Options

With iPadOS 26, app icons are no longer static. You can now select from multiple visual styles:

- **Light Theme Icons** – Brighter, airy icons that suit daylight environments.

- **Dark Theme Icons** – Sleek, shadowed versions ideal for night mode.
- **Tinted Icons** – Choose from a variety of soft color overlays.
- **Clear Icons** – Transparent backgrounds with subtle glowing effects.

To change your icons:

- Tap and hold on the Home Screen > **Edit** > Tap the **three-dot menu** at the bottom > Select **Customize Icons**.

2. Using Widgets with Liquid Glass

Widgets now inherit the Liquid Glass effect:

- They shimmer and blur in the background.
- Widgets dynamically match theme settings.
- Interactive elements like timers, calendars, and music controls update in real time.

3. Folder Enhancements

Folders are no longer bland grey boxes. You can:

- **Add Emojis** to folder labels.
- **Change Folder Colors**.
- **Drag Folders to the Dock** for fast access across apps.

To customize a folder:

- Long press the folder > Tap **Edit Folder** > Choose your color, emoji, or icon style.

4. Smart App Stacks and Grouping

New to iPadOS 26:

- **Dynamic App Stacks**: Similar apps are automatically grouped and displayed in a scrollable format.
- **Smart Suggestions**: iPad intelligently reorders icons based on time of day or activity.

Enable Smart Stacks by holding the Home Screen > tap + > Select **Smart Stack** widget.

5. Wallpaper & Theme Syncing

Wallpapers now interact with the Liquid Glass layer, making every icon and folder appear part of a living canvas. Choose from:

- **Dynamic Wallpapers** that move subtly.
- **Responsive Wallpapers** that change with theme and time.
- **Live Wallpapers** with motion effects.

Set your wallpaper in **Settings > Wallpaper & Home Screen**.

6. Accessibility in Customization

- **Reduce Transparency** to simplify backgrounds.
- **High Contrast** for easier icon recognition.
- **VoiceOver & Haptics** integrated into widget interactions.

Personalization in iPadOS 26 isn't just aesthetic—it's functional. Whether you're simplifying your Home Screen for focus or making it lively for creativity, the new tools let you design a workspace that reflects your personality and supports your workflow.

Control Center and Lock Screen Upgrades

The Control Center and Lock Screen are two of the most frequently accessed areas on the iPad. iPadOS 26 reinvents both, making them more useful, beautiful, and personal.

1. Lock Screen Enhancements

The new Lock Screen isn't just for unlocking your device—it's an information-rich canvas:

- **Customizable Widgets**: Add calendar, fitness rings, notes, battery levels, and more.

- **Interactive Notifications**: Respond to messages, control playback, and complete reminders without unlocking.
- **Face ID Visuals**: A new unlocking animation adds a futuristic glow when Face ID is used.

Changing Lock Screen Layout:

- Go to **Settings > Wallpaper & Lock Screen > Customize**
- Add widgets by tapping the placeholder zones

2. Liquid Glass on Lock Screen

The dynamic reflection and blur from Liquid Glass adds depth to:

- Clock widgets
- Background photos
- Notifications and alerts

3. Control Center Redesign

The Control Center in iPadOS 26 has been overhauled for easier access and greater flexibility:

- **Floating Panels**: Controls float above Liquid Glass for better contrast
- **Custom Tiles**: Add or remove tiles such as Focus Mode, Home controls, Quick Notes, Low Power Mode

- **Grouped Controls**: Audio controls are grouped with AirPlay and spatial audio tools

Accessing and Customizing:

- Swipe down from the top-right corner
- Tap **Edit Controls** at the bottom
- Drag new tools into the panel or rearrange existing ones

4. Audio and Media Widgets

Control Center includes:

- **Expanded Now Playing widget**
- **Voice Isolation toggle**
- **Live Activities** (background downloads, running timers, call status)

5. Security and Privacy Options

- **Lock Screen Access** settings determine which controls (camera, wallet, notifications) are available before unlocking
- **Temporary Disabling of Face ID**: Press and hold power + volume button

6. Useful Additions

- **Quick Journal Entry**: Tap to write a new journal entry without opening the app

- **Preview Scanner Access**: One-tap scanning of PDFs or photos directly from Control Center

7. Accessibility Features

- **Magnifier** and **Hearing Controls** are easier to toggle
- **Voice Control Shortcuts** now show contextual commands

Together, the new Control Center and Lock Screen deliver more control and at-a-glance information without overwhelming the user. Combined with Liquid Glass, they become elegant, intuitive command centers that respond beautifully to every interaction.

With a deeper understanding of iPadOS 26's Liquid Glass design and the visual upgrades it brings to your Home Screen, Lock Screen, and Control Center, you're now ready to explore multitasking, windowing, and pro features that redefine productivity on your iPad in the next chapter.

Chapter 3: The All-New Windowing System

Multitasking Reinvented: Window Resizing, Tiling & Exposé

iPadOS 26 introduces a monumental shift in multitasking capabilities with a brand-new **windowing system** that blends intuitive gestures, dynamic window resizing, and flexible layouts into a productivity powerhouse. This section explores how Apple reinvented multitasking for iPad—offering precision, fluidity, and freedom.

1. The Philosophy of the New Windowing System

Apple's approach with iPadOS 26 is to maintain the **intuitive simplicity** of iPad while introducing powerful new capabilities:

- **Dynamic window resizing**
- **Tiling and snapping** of windows for organized multitasking
- **Exposé** for an aerial view of open apps
- A seamless experience across **touch**, **keyboard**, **trackpad**, and **Apple Pencil**

2. Window Resizing

Users can now **manually resize app windows** by dragging their corners or edges. Here's how to get started:

- Open an app in multitasking mode
- Tap the three-dot menu at the top of the window
- Drag the edges or corners to resize freely

The window will intelligently **snap to suggested sizes**, optimizing layout while keeping it customizable.

3. Tiling Windows with Flick Gestures

Designed specifically for iPad's touch-first nature, **tiling** allows users to:

- **Flick** a window to the side to auto-tile
- **Stack** windows horizontally or vertically
- **Adjust the divider** between tiled windows to change proportions

This means you can now run **multiple instances of the same app** (e.g., two Safari windows side-by-side) or combine different apps like Notes and Files for streamlined workflows.

4. Exposé View

Exposé gives you a zoomed-out view of all open windows for the current app:

- Access it by swiping up from the Dock or using the multitasking gesture
- Tap on the app icon > hold > choose **Show All Windows**
- Easily switch between, rearrange, or close windows

This is especially useful for power users working with multiple documents or browser tabs.

5. Persistent Window Layouts

When you close and reopen a resized app, iPadOS 26 remembers its last configuration:

- Apps **open in the same size and position**
- Tiled layouts are **saved and restored**, creating a more desktop-like continuity

6. Drag & Drop Support

You can now:

- Drag files or images across open windows
- Use split view to copy text from Safari to Notes
- Move entire blocks of content with intuitive gestures

7. Keyboard Shortcuts for Pros

- **Command + Tab**: Switch between apps
- **Control + Down Arrow**: Enter Exposé

- **Globe + Arrow Keys**: Snap windows to corners or sides

Multitasking in iPadOS 26 is a complete reinvention that feels powerful, intuitive, and surprisingly close to a desktop operating system—all while retaining the iPad's signature ease of use.

Using Stage Manager and External Displays

iPadOS 26 builds upon the original **Stage Manager** concept and dramatically enhances it, especially when used with **external displays**. Whether you're a creative pro, a student, or a business user, these features give your iPad a new identity as a serious productivity hub.

1. What is Stage Manager?

Stage Manager is a **windowed multitasking mode** that lets users:

- Arrange and overlap multiple windows
- Group apps into separate "stages" for different tasks
- Use a Mac-like experience with keyboard and pointer

In iPadOS 26, Stage Manager is even more fluid:

- Supports **up to four apps on iPad** and more when connected to a display
- Offers **resizable and overlapping** windows
- Works seamlessly with **drag & drop**, **external keyboard**, and **mouse or trackpad**

2. Getting Started with Stage Manager

To enable Stage Manager:

- Open **Control Center**
- Tap the **Stage Manager** icon
- Drag apps from the Dock or Spotlight into the workspace

You can then resize, overlap, or group apps.

3. Managing Stages

- Each group of apps forms a "stage"
- Switch between stages using the **sidebar**
- Close or modify stages by tapping the top window and dragging out apps

4. Using an External Display

iPadOS 26 offers full native resolution support for external monitors:

- Connect via **USB-C** or **Thunderbolt**
- Display extends your workspace (not mirrored)
- Use separate app arrangements on each screen

5. What You Can Do with an External Display

- Run Photoshop on iPad while previewing images on an external screen
- Use the Files app fullscreen on one screen while referencing Notes on another
- Connect Bluetooth mouse and keyboard for a desktop-like experience

6. App Behavior on External Displays

Apps open in new windows on the external display by default. You can:

- Move windows between displays by dragging
- Use **Exposé** or **Stage Manager** to switch views
- Use the **menu bar** (covered in the next section) to control window actions

7. System Requirements for Stage Manager + External Display

- iPads with **M1 or later** chips support Stage Manager on external displays
- Compatible with iPad Pro 11-inch (3rd gen and later), iPad Air (5th gen and later), iPad Pro 12.9-inch (5th gen and later)

Stage Manager turns your iPad into a multitasking workstation—especially when paired with a large screen and external peripherals. This is iPadOS 26 at its most professional.

Mastering the New Menu Bar

One of the most transformative UI features in iPadOS 26 is the introduction of a **persistent menu bar**, bringing the power of desktop-level app control to iPad.

1. What is the iPad Menu Bar?

The Menu Bar is a new horizontal control strip that appears at the top of the screen when:

- You swipe down from the top
- You hover your cursor at the top (with a trackpad or mouse)

It provides quick access to:

- App menus
- Searchable commands
- Settings and help functions

2. Where the Menu Bar Appears

- Within apps like **Files, Safari, Notes, Pages,** and **Third-Party Apps** that support the new API
- On the **external display**, similar to macOS

3. Navigating the Menu Bar

Menus are context-sensitive:

- **File, Edit, View, Insert**, and other dropdowns depending on the app
- Tap or click to reveal sub-menus
- Long-press or use right-click to reveal quick actions

4. Searchable Commands

At the top-right corner of the Menu Bar is a **search field**:

- Type a keyword to find features or tools (e.g., "Split View", "Print", "Table")
- Tap a result to immediately launch it

5. Developer Integration

Third-party developers can now:

- Add custom actions and shortcuts to the Menu Bar
- Enable contextual dropdowns and search
- Use the new **Menu Bar API** in iPadOS 26 SDK

6. Multitasking Integration

The Menu Bar enhances multitasking:

- Drag a window from the Menu Bar

- Quickly minimize, tile, or close an app from the dropdown options
- Use the bar to switch between open stages or windows

7. Menu Bar and Accessibility

Apple has ensured the Menu Bar is fully accessible:

- **VoiceOver** users can navigate it by swiping
- **Large Text** settings apply
- **Haptic feedback** with external keyboards

8. Tips for Power Users

- **Hold Option** while clicking for alternate actions
- Use **Globe + M** to open the Menu Bar from anywhere
- Assign custom shortcuts in **Settings > Keyboard > Shortcuts**

The Menu Bar in iPadOS 26 unifies the desktop and tablet experience, offering the kind of power and flexibility long craved by iPad power users. It complements multitasking, accelerates workflows, and introduces a new layer of intuitive control.

Together, these innovations—resizable windows, Stage Manager, external display support, and the Menu Bar—form the most significant upgrade to iPad multitasking ever. With Chapter 3 complete, you're now ready to harness the full productivity potential of iPadOS 26 in both work and creative pursuits.

Chapter 4: Apple Intelligence Explained

What Is Apple Intelligence?

With the release of iPadOS 26, Apple has introduced **Apple Intelligence**, a groundbreaking personal intelligence system that sets a new standard in AI integration. Unlike traditional artificial intelligence services that rely heavily on cloud processing and third-party data mining, Apple Intelligence is deeply rooted in the principles of **privacy, contextual awareness**, and **on-device processing**. This section explores what Apple Intelligence is, how it works, and why it's transformative for iPad users.

1. The Core Philosophy Behind Apple Intelligence

Apple Intelligence is not just another AI feature—it represents a fundamental shift in how devices understand and respond to users:

- **Privacy-first architecture**: Data is processed on-device whenever possible.
- **Contextual intelligence**: Apple Intelligence understands what you're doing, what matters most, and when to help.

- **Cross-app awareness**: It integrates seamlessly across iPadOS, from communication to creativity.

2. Key Capabilities of Apple Intelligence

- **Live Translation**: Communicate across languages in real time.
- **Genmoji**: Create AI-generated emojis that reflect unique moods, styles, and personas.
- **Image Playground**: Generate and personalize visuals with prompts, styles, and your own photos.
- **AI-Powered Shortcuts**: Automate tasks based on smart understanding of context and content.

3. How It Works

Apple Intelligence leverages the **Apple Neural Engine** and **Secure Enclave** to perform calculations:

- Data stays local unless you opt to send it to iCloud securely.
- On-device AI models are optimized for power efficiency.
- It operates in harmony with Siri, Safari, Notes, Messages, and third-party apps via new APIs.

4. Why Apple Intelligence Matters

- **Speed**: Real-time responses and minimal latency.

- **Trust**: Apple never builds user profiles for advertising.
- **Accessibility**: AI tools improve productivity for users with disabilities.

5. Supported Devices

Apple Intelligence requires devices with:

- **M1 chip or later** (iPad Pro, iPad Air, iPad mini with A17 Pro)
- Siri and system language set to a supported Apple Intelligence language.

Apple Intelligence redefines what's possible with on-device AI. It empowers users to interact with their iPad in more human, personalized, and meaningful ways—without sacrificing control or privacy.

Using Live Translation in FaceTime, Phone & Messages

One of the most exciting features of Apple Intelligence is **Live Translation**—a systemwide tool that breaks language barriers across FaceTime, Phone, and Messages. In an increasingly globalized world, this feature ensures seamless communication regardless of language.

1. What Is Live Translation?

Live Translation allows users to:

- Instantly translate conversations in real-time.
- Read captions during FaceTime or hear spoken translations on phone calls.
- Translate incoming and outgoing texts in Messages.

2. How to Enable Live Translation

To activate Live Translation:

- Go to **Settings > General > Language & Region**.
- Enable **Live Translation** and set your preferred language.
- For FaceTime and Phone, ensure **Audio & Captions** is turned on in the relevant app settings.

3. Live Translation in FaceTime

When using FaceTime:

- AI-generated **live captions** display at the bottom of the screen.
- Captions update in real-time, preserving tone and meaning.
- You can still hear the speaker's original voice while reading translated text.

This is incredibly useful for international meetings, tutoring, or family calls.

4. Live Translation in Phone Calls

Apple Intelligence offers two modes:

- **Spoken translation**: Your iPad reads aloud your translated response.
- **Bilingual captioning**: You see both original and translated speech during the call.

This is ideal for travel, interviews, or customer support.

5. Live Translation in Messages

- Incoming messages are auto-translated into your preferred language.
- Group messages maintain multilingual context.
- Tap and hold a message to see the original and translated text.

6. Supported Languages

Initially supports:

- English, Spanish, French, German, Italian, Portuguese (Brazil), Chinese (Simplified), Japanese, and Korean.

Planned support includes:

- Dutch, Vietnamese, Turkish, and more by year-end.

7. Use Cases for Live Translation

- **Business**: Negotiate deals, coordinate across departments.
- **Education**: Language tutoring and cultural exchange.
- **Travel**: Communicate with locals and services abroad.

Live Translation brings real-time multilingual communication to your fingertips, bridging cultures without the need for external translation tools.

Creating with Genmoji and Image Playground

iPadOS 26 introduces two standout creative features under Apple Intelligence: **Genmoji** and **Image Playground**. These tools transform how users express themselves visually—whether through personalized emojis or AI-generated art.

1. What is Genmoji?

Genmoji lets users create entirely custom emoji using AI:

- Start with a base emoji (smile, wink, laugh, etc.)
- Add attributes: hairstyle, skin tone, accessories, expressions
- Preview and tweak in real-time

To create a Genmoji:

- Open **Messages > Stickers > Genmoji**
- Tap **Create** and customize your Genmoji

2. Genmoji Use Cases

- Send a personalized version of yourself
- Create inside jokes with friends
- Add flair to business communication

3. What is Image Playground?

Image Playground is an AI image generation tool that lets you:

- Create visuals from scratch using a text prompt
- Upload a reference photo to stylize
- Choose artistic filters (sketch, oil painting, cartoon, etc.)

You can access Image Playground in:

- **Messages**
- **Notes**
- **Mail**
- **Files** (for attaching generated images)

4. Using Prompts and Styles

Image Playground works via prompts:

- "A futuristic city at sunset in watercolor style"
- "A dog in a space suit, Pixar-style"

Then choose:

- **Mood** (whimsical, serious, dreamy)
- **Style** (3D, charcoal, neon)

5. Integration with ChatGPT (via Apple Intelligence)

Some prompts may route through ChatGPT:

- ChatGPT helps refine and enhance images
- No login needed; it's privacy-respecting and session-based

6. AI Ethics and Safety

Apple censors offensive content and ensures safe, inclusive visuals.

7. Creativity Unleashed

- **Educators**: Create flashcards, visual aids
- **Designers**: Generate mockups and style inspiration
- **Social Media Users**: Personalize stories, posts, and reactions

Together, Genmoji and Image Playground empower you to visually express thoughts, feelings, and creativity beyond anything previously possible on iPad.

Smarter Shortcuts with AI-Powered Actions

Apple Intelligence redefines automation in iPadOS 26 by upgrading the **Shortcuts** app with **context-aware, AI-powered actions**. These new capabilities turn your iPad into a truly smart assistant capable of performing personalized tasks at just the right time.

1. What's New in Shortcuts

- **Smart Suggestions**: AI proposes shortcuts based on your habits and app usage.
- **AI Modules**: Tap into Apple Intelligence to summarize, translate, or create content.
- **Shortcut Inputs**: Use voice, touch, or context triggers.

2. Creating Smarter Shortcuts

Start from scratch or choose an AI-powered template:

- Open **Shortcuts**
- Tap + > **New Shortcut** > **Add Action**

- Search "Apple Intelligence" to browse available tools

Examples:

- Summarize notes from a meeting
- Compare a lecture's transcript with your handwritten notes
- Generate an image and send it to a friend

3. Real-Life Use Cases

- **Students**: Automate research, reminders, and study summaries
- **Professionals**: Auto-generate reports or organize files based on time/date
- **Families**: Set up shared grocery lists or morning routines

4. Personalization and Context Awareness

AI-powered shortcuts can:

- Trigger based on location or time of day
- Adjust behavior based on focus mode or calendar events
- Suggest follow-up actions like opening related documents

5. Integration with Other Apps

- Works with Files, Messages, Safari, Calendar, Mail
- Developers can plug into the new Shortcuts API to add AI capabilities

6. Privacy and Data Control

- You choose which data is used
- On-device processing is default
- Prompts can be customized for transparency and control

7. Example Shortcut: Daily Briefing

- 8:00 AM: Summarize unread emails
- Show today's events from Calendar
- Display weather and traffic updates
- Suggest journaling prompt via Notes

8. Exporting and Sharing

- Share shortcuts via iCloud link
- Import from friends or community
- Create shortcut folders in the Dock for fast access

The Shortcuts app in iPadOS 26 now offers real intelligence—responsive, relevant, and refreshingly easy to use. It turns every tap into something smarter.

With Apple Intelligence now demystified, you're equipped to use iPadOS 26 as a hyper-personal, context-aware digital assistant and creative partner. Up next: explore how iPadOS enhances your productivity through powerful file management and new app capabilities.

Chapter 5: Power Productivity Tools

New Features in the Files App

iPadOS 26 brings a major overhaul to the **Files app**, transforming it into a powerful file management tool that rivals desktop-level systems. Whether you're a student managing documents, a professional juggling client folders, or a creative working with media files, the new Files app streamlines your workflows like never before.

1. Revamped Interface and Navigation

- The new **List View** adds a desktop-like feel with resizable columns and collapsible folders.
- **Multi-select** and **drag-and-drop** are now smoother and faster.
- Improved sidebar navigation groups folders by recency, favorites, and tags.

2. Dynamic File Previews

- Tap and hold to instantly preview documents, images, or videos without opening a new window.

- Enhanced media previews let you scrub through video clips or flip through multi-page PDFs directly in Files.

3. Improved Search and Filters

- **Smart Search** now includes content-aware results, letting you search within file contents.
- Filter results by file type, date, app used, or tags with new dropdown menus.
- Auto-suggestions help refine results dynamically as you type.

4. Integration with Apple Intelligence

- Use AI to summarize documents or extract data from PDFs directly in the preview pane.
- Smart tags are auto-suggested based on file content and history.

5. Enhanced File Sharing and Permissions

- Share files with expiring links or password protection.
- Control permissions (view-only, edit, comment) more granularly.
- Real-time collaboration features now include typing indicators and change history.

6. Files App for Power Users

- Use keyboard shortcuts like **Command + N** to create a new folder.
- Access recently closed documents via the new "History" tab.
- Batch rename files and folders using custom naming patterns.

The new Files app in iPadOS 26 bridges the gap between mobile simplicity and professional-level productivity.

Folder Customization and Dock Integration

One of the most welcomed additions to the iPadOS 26 Files ecosystem is deep **folder customization** and the ability to add folders directly to the **Dock** for quicker access. These features offer not only better organization but also faster navigation across workspaces.

1. Visual Folder Customization

- Choose from **custom icons**, emojis, or images to visually differentiate folders.
- Apply **color labels** or gradients to folders.
- Customize folder previews to show recent items or a static thumbnail.

2. How to Customize a Folder

- Long-press on a folder and select **Customize**.
- Choose an icon, assign a label color, and add emoji or title stickers.
- Tap **Done** to apply across all views.

3. Syncing Customizations Across Devices

- Custom folders sync via iCloud, appearing exactly the same on iPhone, iPad, and Mac.
- Changes are instant and platform-consistent.

4. Adding Folders to the Dock

- Drag and drop any folder from the Files app into the iPad Dock.
- The folder remains pinned for quick access—even from within other apps.
- Tap the Docked folder to open a compact overlay version of Files.

5. Organizing the Dock

- Combine folders with app icons for grouped workflows (e.g., a folder of PDFs next to Preview).
- Use divider spacing or empty icons (via Shortcuts) for cleaner Dock layouts.

6. Use Cases for Dock Integration

- **Students**: Pin a folder with course notes, slides, and recordings.

- **Professionals**: Keep a client folder docked for access during Zoom calls or document editing.
- **Designers**: Store assets, design references, and brand kits together.

7. Tips for Power Users

- Create Dock folders filled with app-specific templates.
- Use Focus Mode to show different Dock folders based on time or location.
- Set up automation via Shortcuts to change folder appearance when switching tasks.

Folder customization and Dock integration take the visual and functional experience of iPad file management to an entirely new level—empowering you to work faster, smarter, and with style.

Setting Default Apps for File Types

iPadOS 26 finally brings a long-requested feature: the ability to **set default apps for file types**. Whether you prefer a third-party PDF reader, an advanced text editor, or a design-specific image viewer, you can now take full control of how files open on your iPad.

1. Why Default Apps Matter

- Eliminates the repetitive task of selecting apps manually.
- Improves workflow speed by instantly launching files with your preferred tool.
- Enables custom behavior for different tasks (e.g., editing in one app, viewing in another).

2. How to Set a Default App

- Long-press a file and choose **Info** > **Open With**.
- Select **Set as Default for This File Type**.
- iPadOS will remember your choice across sessions and devices.

3. File Types Supported

- PDF, DOCX, TXT, CSV, HTML, MP4, JPEG, PNG, ZIP, and more.
- Developers can register their apps as compatible handlers for specific extensions.

4. Managing Defaults in Settings

- Navigate to **Settings** > **Files** > **Default Apps**.
- View and change associations per file type.
- Restore to system default if needed.

5. Integration with iCloud and Shortcuts

- Default app choices sync via iCloud.

- Combine with Shortcuts to trigger app behavior when opening a specific type (e.g., always edit PDFs with GoodReader and then email via Mail).

6. Power User Customizations

- Set different default apps based on **Focus Mode** (e.g., work vs. personal).
- Use Automations to temporarily change default apps during certain activities.

7. Example Workflow

- A writer can open DOCX files with Microsoft Word and TXT files with iA Writer.
- A photographer might default to Affinity Photo for images and Dropbox for ZIPs.
- A student could use Notability for PDFs and Numbers for spreadsheets.

8. Security and Privacy

- Apps must request permission to open file types.
- Sandbox protections still apply—your files remain secure.

Default app settings mark a significant leap forward in personalization and productivity on iPad. Combined with the other power features in iPadOS 26, they ensure your device works exactly the way you want it to.

In Chapter 5, we've unlocked the full power of iPad's productivity enhancements in iPadOS 26. Up next: discover how creatives can take their audio, video, and document workflows to the next level with new content creation tools.

Chapter 6: Mastering the Preview App

Viewing and Editing PDFs and Images

iPadOS 26 brings the long-awaited **Preview app** to the iPad, introducing a robust and flexible toolset for viewing, editing, and managing PDF documents and images. This addition transforms the iPad into a true productivity machine, especially for students, professionals, and creatives who work with visual content or documents on a regular basis.

1. Introduction to Preview on iPad

Previously available only on macOS, Preview is now a native iPad app that integrates seamlessly with the Files app, Markup tools, and Apple Pencil. It allows users to:

- Open and view PDFs, images, and scanned documents.
- Annotate documents using Apple Pencil or touch.
- Rearrange, delete, or add PDF pages.
- Sign forms, highlight content, and export documents in multiple formats.

2. Opening Files in Preview

- Open the **Files app**, locate your document or image.
- Tap once to open in Preview (set as default for PDFs/images).
- Alternatively, open Preview directly and browse your documents.

3. Viewing PDFs

- Use swipe gestures or the navigation pane to flip through pages.
- Tap on thumbnails to jump to a specific page.
- Enable **two-page view** or **scrolling view** for easier reading.

4. Viewing and Managing Images

- Supported formats include JPG, PNG, HEIC, TIFF, and more.
- View metadata, resolution, and size by tapping **Info**.
- Zoom, rotate, or crop using intuitive gestures or the editing toolbar.

5. Editing PDFs

- Tap **Edit** to rearrange pages by dragging thumbnails.
- Add new pages from templates, blank pages, or scans.
- Delete unwanted pages or duplicate key sections.

6. Combining and Splitting PDFs

- Drag a PDF into another PDF within Preview to merge.
- Use **Split View** to open two PDFs and copy pages between them.
- Save a range of selected pages as a new file.

7. Export and Share Options

- Export in PDF, JPG, or PNG formats.
- Optimize file size or quality.
- Use the **Share Sheet** to send files via Mail, AirDrop, or save to Files.

8. Integration with iCloud Drive

- All changes are auto-saved and synced across devices.
- Access your edited files from any Apple device.

With Preview on iPad, working with PDFs and images is more efficient, intuitive, and integrated into your daily workflows.

Using Markup with Apple Pencil

Markup is the secret power behind the Preview app—and when paired with the **Apple Pencil**, it becomes a versatile and precise tool for annotation, drawing, and note-taking directly within documents.

1. Launching Markup in Preview

- Open a PDF or image in Preview.
- Tap the **Markup** icon (pen tip) in the toolbar.
- The full markup suite appears at the bottom of the screen.

2. Apple Pencil Integration

- Apple Pencil provides fluid, natural writing and drawing.
- Use pressure and tilt sensitivity for precision.
- Scribble to convert handwriting into text in supported fields.

3. Available Markup Tools

- **Pen**, **Pencil**, and **Highlighter**: Draw, write, or highlight.
- **Eraser**: Remove specific strokes or entire sections.
- **Lasso Tool**: Move or copy markup content.
- **Shapes**: Add arrows, boxes, circles, and lines.
- **Text Tool**: Insert text boxes for typed annotations.
- **Signature Tool**: Sign documents with stored or drawn signatures.

4. Advanced Features with PencilKit

- App developers can tap into the **PencilKit API** for deeper integration.
- Use custom brushes, pressure-based tools, or interactive annotations.
- In Freeform or Notes, Markup even adapts to writing styles.

5. Use Cases for Markup with Apple Pencil

- **Students**: Highlight passages, circle keywords, or annotate lecture slides.
- **Professionals**: Review contracts, sign forms, or add comments to reports.
- **Creatives**: Sketch on images, storyboard scenes, or mock up UI designs.

6. Saving and Exporting Marked-Up Files

- All edits are non-destructive; you can revert to the original.
- Share annotated files directly or save a flattened copy.

7. Accessibility and Pen Options

- Markup supports **VoiceOver**, **Zoom**, and **Color Filters**.
- Use **Double-Tap on Pencil (2nd gen)** to switch between tools.

Markup in Preview, especially when paired with Apple Pencil, turns the iPad into a paperless productivity powerhouse.

AutoFill and Creating Quick Sketches

Beyond viewing and annotating, Preview introduces smart form handling with **AutoFill**, and the ability to make **quick sketches**—offering a complete solution for paperwork, design, and creativity on the go.

1. Using AutoFill in PDFs

- Preview detects form fields automatically.
- Tap on a field and suggested entries appear above the keyboard.
- Use **AutoFill** to insert contact information, email, phone number, address, etc.
- Stored information is securely pulled from your Contacts and iCloud Keychain.

2. Customizing AutoFill Entries

- Go to **Settings > Safari > AutoFill**.
- Add or edit personal details.
- Preview syncs this data across Apple apps securely.

3. Signing Forms with AutoFill

- Tap the **Signature Tool**.
- Select an existing signature or create a new one.
- Drag and drop the signature to the required field.
- Adjust size and position with gestures.

4. Creating Quick Sketches

- Tap + > **Add Page** > **Blank Page** inside Preview.
- Use Apple Pencil or finger to sketch ideas, diagrams, or illustrations.
- Combine sketches with text boxes, shapes, and arrows.

5. Sketch Use Cases

- **Business**: Whiteboard ideas, org charts, and visual notes.
- **Art & Design**: Draft concepts, layout scenes, or develop characters.
- **Education**: Draw maps, timelines, or annotate diagrams.

6. Sharing Sketches

- Export as image or PDF.
- Add to presentations or upload to cloud storage.
- Drag into Notes, Pages, or Freeform for extended workflows.

7. Templates and Creative Tools

- Choose from lined, dotted, or grid backgrounds.
- Use templates for storyboarding, forms, or planner layouts.

8. Tips for Better Sketching

- Use the **lasso tool** to rearrange parts of your sketch.
- Enable **Snap to Grid** for cleaner lines.
- Use **Color Picker** and **opacity sliders** for shading effects.

Whether you're quickly signing a document, filling out a form, or sketching a rough idea, Preview's AutoFill and sketching features simplify and speed up your workflow without the need for third-party apps.

In Chapter 6, you've learned how to harness the full potential of Preview—turning your iPad into a digital canvas, a form-filling assistant, and a powerful PDF editor. Coming up next, we'll explore how iPadOS 26 enhances audio and video workflows for creators and professionals alike.

Chapter 7: Audio, Video, and Creative Workflows

Background Tasks for Pro Users

One of the most impactful additions in iPadOS 26 for professional creators is **Background Tasks**. This feature brings desktop-class multitasking to the iPad, enabling users to run intensive processes without being forced to keep the app in the foreground. Whether you're rendering a video, exporting large audio files, or syncing a massive project folder, Background Tasks ensures that your productivity flows uninterrupted.

1. What Are Background Tasks?

Background Tasks refer to operations that continue to run even when the user switches away from the initiating app. Prior to iPadOS 26, many apps would pause these processes as soon as the app was minimized. Now, developers can mark specific tasks as eligible to continue in the background, provided they comply with Apple's new Background Task API.

2. Key Use Cases

- **Video Rendering**: Export a high-resolution video while checking email or browsing.

- **Audio Processing**: Mix and export tracks in Logic Pro or GarageBand.

- **Cloud Syncing**: Upload gigabytes of data to iCloud, Dropbox, or Google Drive.

- **Data Analysis**: Run computational scripts or batch edits in productivity tools.

3. Managing Background Tasks with Live Activities

When a background process begins, iPadOS 26 displays a **Live Activity** in the Dynamic Island (on supported models) or as a persistent notification:

- Tap the notification to return to the app.

- Pause or cancel the task directly from the activity window.

- View estimated completion time, progress, and other stats.

4. Developer Integration

App developers can take advantage of the **Background Tasks API**, which includes:

- Energy efficiency controls
- User-initiated task tracking
- Completion handlers and fallback alerts

These APIs are designed to ensure tasks don't drain your battery or hog memory resources.

5. Custom User Control

You can manage task permissions in:

- **Settings > General > Background Activity**
- Enable/disable background tasks per app
- Set data/wifi preferences to optimize performance

6. Real-World Productivity Gains

- **Creators**: Export multiple projects simultaneously

- **Developers**: Compile and test code without staying locked to one app

- **Photographers**: Auto-enhance or batch convert RAW files

7. Accessibility and Notifications

- Background Tasks are voiceover-compatible

- Receive haptic or banner notifications on task completion

- Sound alerts can be enabled for specific task types

Background Tasks take the iPad from a media consumption tool to a **powerful creation hub**, matching macOS in capability while preserving the intuitive iPadOS experience.

New Audio Input Options and Voice Isolation

iPadOS 26 dramatically expands audio capabilities, giving users **greater control over input sources**, **voice clarity**, and **recording fidelity**. Whether you're a podcaster, musician, student, or journalist, these updates simplify your workflow while improving the quality of your content.

1. Audio Input Per App and Website

Users can now select specific microphones for individual apps and even websites:

- Go to **Settings > Privacy & Security > Microphone Access**

- Select an app or Safari website

- Choose input: internal mic, external USB mic, AirPods mic, etc.

This is especially useful for:

- Switching between a **studio mic** for recording and a **headset mic** for calls

- Using different audio profiles in separate creative apps

2. App-Specific Use Cases

- **GarageBand**: Use an XLR mic with a USB-C interface

- **Safari**: Record feedback on websites like Loom or Google Meet

- **Voice Memos**: Capture personal thoughts with a lavalier mic

3. Voice Isolation for Crystal Clear Audio

Voice Isolation, previously available on macOS and iPhone, now debuts on iPad:

- Filters out background noise in real-time

- Focuses on the user's voice while suppressing ambient sound

Enable in:

- **Control Center > Mic Mode > Voice Isolation**

- Compatible with FaceTime, Zoom, WhatsApp, and other VoIP apps

4. How Voice Isolation Works

Apple uses **machine learning** and the **Neural Engine** to:

- Analyze your vocal frequencies

- Suppress wind, fans, crowds, and traffic noise

- Boost speech clarity while preserving natural tone

5. Compatible Devices

Voice Isolation works best on:

- **iPad Pro (M1 and later)**

- **iPad Air (M2 and later)**

- **iPad mini (A17 Pro)**

- With **AirPods Pro (2nd gen)** or any certified external mic

6. Multi-Mic and Stereo Options

Some apps now support stereo recording and dual-mic capture:

- Record two people using left/right channels

- Perfect for interviews, vlogging, or music duets

7. Audio Monitoring and Mixing

- Preview your mic feed before hitting record
- Adjust gain, EQ, and effects in real-time
- Integrates with Logic Pro and Ferrite for advanced mixing

8. Privacy and Permissions

- Get granular control over app access to mics
- Temporary access options for one-time recordings
- Mic icon appears in status bar when active

These enhancements bring studio-level control to everyday users, eliminating the need for third-party hardware or apps in many workflows.

Using Local Capture for High-Quality Recordings

A major step forward in iPadOS 26's media capabilities is **Local Capture**. This feature allows users to record

high-quality video and audio from any app, even during live video calls. Think of it as your personal content production studio built right into iPadOS.

1. What Is Local Capture?

Local Capture enables recording:

- The user's video and voice feed locally during a call
- Audio from both the user and other participants
- Screen content if permission is granted

It's especially useful for:

- Podcasts
- Online courses
- Interviews
- Professional documentation

2. How to Use Local Capture

When using a compatible app (Zoom, FaceTime, Microsoft Teams):

- Tap the **Local Capture** icon (camera with dot)

- Choose what to record: camera feed, screen, mic input, or all

- Confirm permissions and storage location

3. Quality Settings and Formats

- Video up to **4K at 60fps**, if supported

- Audio: Lossless WAV or compressed AAC

- Optional HDR capture for better visuals

4. Echo Cancellation and Audio Processing

During calls, iPadOS automatically applies:

- **Echo cancellation** to prevent feedback from speakers

- **Voice Isolation** to separate background noise from speech

- **Dynamic Range Compression** for balanced audio levels

5. Storage and File Management

- Files are stored in **Files > Local Capture** by default
- Rename, organize, or move files immediately after recording
- Auto-sync to iCloud or external storage

6. Editing and Exporting

- Open recordings in **iMovie, Final Cut Pro for iPad, or LumaFusion**
- Trim, add transitions, captions, or effects
- Export for YouTube, podcast platforms, or internal use

7. Privacy Controls

- Participants are notified when Local Capture is active
- Encrypted storage options for sensitive content
- Parental controls can restrict access to Local Capture

8. Real-World Use Cases

- **Educators**: Record lectures or tutoring sessions for reuse

- **Journalists**: Capture interviews with sources on the fly

- **Entrepreneurs**: Create explainer videos or customer demos

9. Integration with Third-Party Tools

- Use with Notability for audio/video note capture

- Connect to OBS or Streamlabs for live streaming workflows

- Export directly to Adobe Premiere or DaVinci Resolve

10. Accessibility and Control

- Subtitles auto-generated via Apple Intelligence

- Visual/audio indicators for users with hearing impairments

Local Capture closes the gap between casual users and pros, giving everyone the ability to create polished, broadcast-quality media directly from their iPad.

Chapter 7 has shown how iPadOS 26 elevates content creation and professional workflows with unprecedented support for background tasks, audio enhancements, and powerful media capture tools.

➡️ Chapter 8: Communication Upgraded

Using the New Phone App on iPad

With iPadOS 26, Apple has taken a major step forward in unifying the iPhone and iPad experience by bringing the **Phone app** to iPad for the first time. This seemingly simple addition is a massive leap in terms of functionality and convenience, especially for users who prefer working on the larger screen of an iPad without constantly switching back and forth to their iPhone. In this section, we'll explore how the new Phone app works on iPad, its features, and how to get the most out of it.

A Seamless Cross-Device Experience

Apple's ecosystem has always emphasized continuity, allowing users to start tasks on one device and finish on another. With the Phone app on iPad, this experience becomes even more fluid. Once configured with **Wi-Fi Calling** and **iCloud sync**, users can **make and receive phone calls directly from their iPad** using their iPhone's cellular connection—or, if supported, even directly via eSIM.

This eliminates the need to pick up your iPhone while working, watching videos, or even while using a stylus to design something. Everything from dialling a number to managing call history now happens within the native **Phone app UI** on the iPad.

Setting It Up

Setting up the Phone app on iPadOS 26 is straightforward:

1. **Sign into the same Apple ID** on both your iPhone and iPad.

2. On your iPhone, go to **Settings > Phone > Calls on Other Devices**, and enable your iPad.

3. Make sure **FaceTime is also enabled** on both devices for seamless calling.

4. You can also enable **Wi-Fi Calling**, if your carrier supports it, to make calls without a nearby iPhone.

Once enabled, your iPad gains full access to your contacts, recent calls, favorites, and voicemail.

Hold Assist and Call Screening

With iPadOS 26, Apple introduces **Hold Assist**, a feature powered by Apple Intelligence. If you're placed on hold during a call, Hold Assist can monitor the call in the background and notify you when a real human returns to the line. It's an excellent productivity feature, allowing you to multitask while you wait without missing anything important.

Call Screening, another Apple Intelligence enhancement, helps filter spam or unknown calls. When a call comes in from an unknown number, the iPad can provide a real-time transcript of what the caller is saying before you answer. This gives users more control over which calls are worth their attention and reduces the likelihood of answering scam calls.

Visual Voicemail and Messages Integration

The Phone app on iPad also integrates tightly with **Messages and FaceTime**. Voicemails are transcribed using on-device AI for privacy and are instantly viewable. From the voicemail screen, you can:

- Play the voicemail

- Read the AI-generated transcript

- Share the voicemail via Messages or Notes

- Tap to return the call or respond via text

This integration creates a communication hub right on the iPad, ideal for professionals, students, and creatives.

Messages Overhaul: Backgrounds, Polls & Apple Cash

The **Messages app in iPadOS 26** receives one of its most significant updates in years, making communication more expressive, collaborative, and functional. Whether you're chatting with friends or coordinating with a team, the new enhancements help bring your messages to life.

Conversation Backgrounds

A standout feature in iPadOS 26 is **Conversation Backgrounds**, allowing users to personalize each chat with custom visuals. You can set different backgrounds for different contacts or groups using:

- Solid colors
- Dynamic patterns

- Images from your library

- AI-generated art via Image Playground

These backgrounds aren't just aesthetic; they react to the content of conversations. For instance, a background might animate subtly during a birthday greeting or change color in response to emoji reactions.

Polls in Group Chats

Group chats now support **native polling**, making it easy to gather opinions or vote on plans:

- Create a poll directly within the chat

- Add multiple options

- Allow single or multiple selections

- See results in real-time

Whether it's choosing where to eat, voting on a project decision, or planning an event, this feature eliminates the need for third-party apps or awkward message chains.

Redesigned Details View

The **Details screen** in Messages now serves as a rich dashboard:

- See all **shared media**, links, and documents
- Access **pinned messages**
- Review **location sharing**
- Use built-in **search** to find specific messages or attachments

This redesign is perfect for power users or professionals managing multiple chats. Everything you need is in one place, neatly organized.

Typing Indicators & Reactions

Apple also improves group messaging flow with:

- **Typing indicators** for multiple users in the same group chat
- Improved emoji reactions and **Tapback+**, which lets you react using any emoji
- Quicker message replies and **threaded messages**, even in busy group chats

Apple Cash Requests & Transfers

Money is now a part of the messaging ecosystem. With iPadOS 26:

- Users can **send or request money** via Apple Cash

- Tap to **approve payments** with Face ID

- Set up **recurring transfers** or split bills in a group chat

Apple has also added auto-generated prompts when discussing money—e.g., if someone mentions "I'll pay you back," Messages may suggest sending or requesting cash.

FaceTime Enhancements and Call Features

FaceTime in iPadOS 26 becomes smarter, smoother, and more powerful, both in casual and professional use cases. Leveraging Apple Intelligence and tighter integration with the iPad's audio and video system, FaceTime is now more engaging than ever.

Live Translation with Captions

The headline upgrade is **Live Translation**, which brings real-time captioning and language translation during FaceTime calls. Here's how it works:

- Captions appear at the bottom of the screen while maintaining live audio.

- You can select your spoken language and the language you want to see.

- It supports both one-on-one and group calls.

This is a game-changer for international communication, online learning, remote interviews, and more. Translations are private, handled on-device when possible, or securely in the cloud.

New Video Effects and Presentation Tools

FaceTime adds **Video Reactions** like confetti, fireworks, and thumbs-up animations—but the real value lies in professional enhancements:

- **Presenter Mode**: Let's you share your screen or app window while keeping your face visible in a smaller bubble.

- **Spotlight Focus**: Auto-detects who's speaking and subtly highlights their video.

- **New Backgrounds**: Use AI-generated or camera-blurred backgrounds for a more polished look.

Voice Isolation and Microphone Control

Thanks to new microphone input settings across iPadOS 26, FaceTime now lets you:

- Choose from **Voice Isolation**, **Wide Spectrum**, or **Standard Mic**

- Set different input devices (e.g., AirPods mic vs. iPad mic)

- Maintain high-quality sound even in noisy environments

This improves every FaceTime use case—from podcast interviews to family chats.

FaceTime on External Displays

For iPads that support **external displays** via Stage Manager, FaceTime can now:

- Show video feeds on a secondary screen

- Split views between shared content and video tiles

- Take advantage of wide camera angles using **Center Stage**

This makes the iPad a legitimate conferencing hub for business users.

Final Thoughts

Apple has taken major strides in **enhancing how we communicate** across iPad with iPadOS 26. With a fully-featured Phone app, a richer Messages experience, and smarter, more powerful FaceTime tools, iPad becomes more than a productivity machine—it becomes a central communication powerhouse.

■ Chapter 9: Journaling, Gaming, and Daily Life

Using the Journal App for Wellness and Reflection

The introduction of the **Journal app** on iPadOS 26 brings a deeply personal, powerful tool to users looking to track their mental well-being, reflect on experiences, and engage in meaningful self-expression. With journaling increasingly recognized as a valuable mental health practice, Apple's new offering aims to make it more accessible, intuitive, and inspiring—especially on the larger canvas of the iPad.

Why Journaling Matters

Numerous studies show that journaling can:

- **Reduce stress and anxiety**
- **Improve emotional regulation**

- **Strengthen memory and comprehension**

- **Boost overall mental clarity and mindfulness**

iPadOS 26 taps into these benefits by delivering a journaling tool that combines the emotional depth of handwritten notes with the multimedia richness of Apple's ecosystem.

An Interface Designed for Reflection

The **Journal app** offers a minimal yet elegant interface that focuses on content and mood. Users are greeted by:

- A customizable **dashboard of entries**

- A **calendar view** for tracking daily logs

- Tagging tools and mood indicators

- A search bar to browse entries by keyword, media, or feeling

The app supports **split-view multitasking**, making it easier to reflect while referencing other apps like Safari, Photos, or Notes.

Personalization and Prompts

To combat writer's block and help users form a daily habit, the app includes **daily journaling prompts**. These can be based on:

- Recent photos taken
- Calendar events
- Music you've listened to
- Workouts completed
- Locations visited

Apple Intelligence ensures the prompts are **contextual and relevant**, often asking reflective questions like, "How did this event make you feel?" or "What did you learn today?"

Users can also **bookmark their favorite entries**, **color-code** them, and group journal entries by theme (e.g., gratitude, goals, dreams).

Multimedia Integration

Journaling isn't limited to words:

- **Photos and videos** can be inserted into entries directly from the camera roll.

- **Audio notes** can be recorded using the iPad's built-in mic or AirPods.

- **Drawings and sketches** can be made using **Apple Pencil**, adding a creative, tactile element to the process.

This multimodal approach transforms journaling into a **personal storytelling experience**, letting you document your life visually and audibly, not just in text.

Wellness-First Features

The Journal app integrates seamlessly with Apple's **Health and Mindfulness** tools:

- Users can log moods alongside entries.

- Set **daily journaling reminders** for morning or evening.

- Visualize emotional trends over time using **data insights** from the Health app.

- Use **Face ID or Touch ID** to lock private entries or entire journals.

For those dealing with stress, depression, or major life transitions, the Journal app becomes a **therapeutic anchor**—a safe, secure place to process emotions.

Organizing Multiple Journals

Another key feature is the ability to **create multiple journals** within the app, such as:

- A **work journal** for logging project thoughts
- A **fitness journal** for tracking goals
- A **gratitude journal** for boosting positivity
- A **travel journal** for vacation reflections

Each journal can be themed, tagged, and personalized with custom icons or cover photos, adding emotional weight to the digital experience.

Conclusion

With its combination of **AI-assisted prompts**, **multimedia support**, and **mental wellness integration**, the Journal app on iPadOS 26 goes far beyond traditional note-taking. It becomes an emotional compass, a wellness tracker, and a canvas for creative self-expression—all in one.

Exploring the New Apple Games App and Game Overlay

For years, gaming on iPad has been limited to individual titles and Game Center—until now. With iPadOS 26, Apple introduces the all-new **Apple Games app**, finally giving iPad users a centralized hub for discovering, managing, and enhancing their gaming experience. Paired with the new **Game Overlay**, this is a transformative upgrade for mobile gamers.

A Hub for All Your Games

The **Apple Games app** is designed to function as your **digital game library**, similar to platforms like Steam or Xbox Game Pass:

- All installed and cloud-synced games are displayed in one interface.

- Games can be **sorted** by genre, playtime, recently played, or controller support.

- **Achievements**, **leaderboards**, and **game stats** are tracked automatically.

There is also **deep integration** with Game Center, including:

- Real-time friend activity

- Party invitations

- Shared gameplay clips

Users can also discover new games through **editorial content**, curated collections, and trending charts.

Introducing Game Overlay

Multitasking during gaming has historically been clunky on mobile platforms. Apple solves this with **Game Overlay**—a floating UI layer that brings critical functions within reach without disrupting gameplay.

Features include:

- **Quick access to chats and messages**

- Real-time **frame rate and battery usage stats**

- **Record gameplay** or take screenshots

- Invite friends or join multiplayer matches

- View game-specific events, like limited-time challenges

You can move or hide the overlay with gestures, ensuring it never obstructs gameplay.

Controller and Cross-Platform Support

Apple continues to support console-quality experiences by enhancing:

- **Bluetooth controller support** (PS5, Xbox, and third-party)
- Low-latency connections
- Vibration feedback
- Button mapping customization

iCloud syncing now works seamlessly across Apple devices, meaning you can **start a game on iPad, continue on Mac**, and **chat via iPhone**—all while remaining logged in.

AI-Enhanced Game Discovery

Apple Intelligence powers **recommendation engines** within the Apple Games app. Based on your play history, game reviews, and social trends, the app can suggest:

- Games you're likely to enjoy

- DLCs and expansion packs for games you already own

- Scheduled events and community updates

This AI-driven discovery process makes it **easier to find hidden gems** without digging through the App Store.

Game Streaming and Replay

Although Apple has historically been cautious with cloud gaming, iPadOS 26 offers:

- **Replay support** to record, trim, and share key gameplay moments

- Screen recording tools compatible with Twitch and YouTube

- Optional **streaming overlays** with camera input (ideal for content creators)

Game Replay lets players showcase achievements, tutorials, or funny moments—and share them via AirDrop, iMessage, or external platforms.

Conclusion

The introduction of the Apple Games app and Game Overlay is a major milestone in making the iPad a **first-class gaming device**. From controller support to AI discovery, Apple is clearly positioning iPad as a **versatile gaming platform** suitable for casual and serious gamers alike.

Integrating Journal with Maps, Audio, and Media

The iPad's strength lies in its ability to merge **apps and features** into unified workflows, and the Journal app is no exception. With iPadOS 26, Apple has deeply integrated **Maps, audio, and media** to allow users to craft journal entries that are **location-rich, emotionally resonant, and multimedia-driven**.

Location Data and Map Integration

Thanks to location services and **Apple Maps**, the Journal app can automatically log where you were when you created an entry. But it goes further:

- View past entries on a **map timeline**.

- Pin favorite entries to specific places.

- See trends—e.g., journaling habits based on location (home, gym, travel, etc.).

This is particularly useful for:

- **Travelers**, who want a visual journal of their journey.

- **Students**, who can track study environments.

- **Therapists or coaches**, who want to analyze emotional state vs. environment.

Users can add **routes** or **landmarks** to entries for richer storytelling.

Audio Integration

Whether recording your own voice, saving a conversation, or attaching a favorite song, the Journal app allows:

- **Audio logs** via built-in mic or AirPods

- **Transcribed recordings** powered by Apple Intelligence

- Attach **Apple Music** tracks that relate to your day or mood

This creates an **immersive experience**, turning each entry into an audio diary.

Example use cases:

- Capture the **sound of waves** during a beach walk.
- Record your child's first words.
- Save voice notes from a therapy session or brainstorming session.

Media & Memory Curation

Apple Photos integration lets you:

- Attach images and videos with one tap.
- Pull in **Memories** generated by iOS.
- Use **Live Photos** for movement and emotion.
- Apply **Image Playground** AI to create illustrations or cover art.

Journal entries can include:

- **Mood tags**

- **Media sliders**

- **Photo descriptions** (written manually or with AI help)

The result is a **living, breathing timeline** of your life, enriched by context and creativity.

Conclusion

By combining Journal with **Maps, audio, and media**, iPadOS 26 turns simple reflections into rich narratives. It empowers users to **capture, understand, and reflect on their lives** in ways that are deeply personal, immersive, and beautifully organized.

👆 Chapter 10: Math, Notes, and Calligraphy

Math Notes and 3D Graphing in Calculator

One of the most academically transformative updates in **iPadOS 26** is the evolution of the **Calculator app**, which now includes **Math Notes** and **3D graphing capabilities**. Once considered a basic utility, the Calculator has transformed into a powerhouse for students, engineers, educators, and anyone who needs dynamic computation support on iPad.

Introduction to Math Notes

Math Notes in iPadOS 26 brings handwriting recognition and live calculation together. It allows users to:

- **Write mathematical expressions** using Apple Pencil or touch

- See instant **real-time results** as you write

- Use natural math notation, such as square roots, exponents, fractions, and even logarithms

- Tap to convert handwritten equations into **typed text**

This means you can now **write math like you think it**, without switching between handwriting and keyboards.

Use Cases for Different Users

Students can write formulas during lectures, get instant results, and save entire sessions to Notes or Files. For example:

- Calculating algebraic expressions like $x2+2x+1x^2 + 2x + 1$

- Solving calculus problems like $\int x2dx \int x^2 \, dx$

- Working on trigonometric identities

Educators benefit by demonstrating problems live, using Apple Pencil and sharing screens via AirPlay during presentations or remote learning.

Scientists and engineers can use it for quick estimations and model testing, including complex operations like:

- Differential equations
- Scientific notation
- Matrix multiplication

All notes are **searchable** and can be exported to PDF, shared via Messages, or stored in iCloud Drive.

Introducing 3D Graphing

One of the most exciting features of the new Calculator app is **3D graphing**, making iPad a visual math lab:

- Users can graph equations with **three variables** such as z=x2+y2z = x^2 + y^2
- Rotate and scale the graphs with **multitouch gestures**
- View cross-sections and slices of surfaces
- Customize axes, color schemes, and grids

This opens new doors in:

- **Multivariable calculus**
- **Linear algebra and geometry**

- **Physics simulations**

- **Data visualization for STEM fields**

The **3D viewer** is fluid, intuitive, and interactive. You can pause rotation, mark coordinates, and export screenshots for reports or presentations.

Smart Recognition and Apple Intelligence

Apple Intelligence supports **math recognition** through smart OCR and language understanding:

- Mistyped or miswritten characters are corrected automatically

- Suggestions are provided to continue solving or simplifying

- Long expressions can be broken down step by step

For example, typing "Find the derivative of 3x3−2x+53x^3 - 2x + 5" will show both the solution and the intermediate steps.

Integration Across Apps

Math Notes can be:

- **Pinned** inside the Notes app

- Dragged into Pages documents or Keynote

- Converted into LaTeX or Markdown

- Saved as PDFs or images for annotations

This makes it perfect for **report writing, homework**, and **real-time tutoring**.

Conclusion

With **Math Notes** and **3D graphing**, the Calculator app on iPadOS 26 becomes a central tool for **education, research, and problem-solving**. Whether you're a high school student, college professor, or data analyst, this feature makes iPad a full-fledged math lab in your hands.

Using Markdown in Notes

The **Notes app** in iPadOS 26 takes a significant leap forward by adding **native Markdown support**, transforming it into a robust writing and coding companion. Markdown is a lightweight markup language used for formatting text using simple, human-readable syntax—ideal for developers, bloggers, students, and professional writers alike.

What is Markdown and Why It Matters

Markdown allows you to format text with simple symbols:

- `#` for headers

- `**bold**` or `_italic_`

- `-` or `*` for bullet lists

- `[ ] ( )` for links

By using Markdown, users can **focus on writing**, without needing complex formatting menus or toggles. It's fast, readable, and highly portable.

New Markdown Features in iPadOS 26 Notes

Apple has now brought Markdown directly into **Notes**, meaning:

- **Live previewing** of Markdown as you type

- Toggle between **code view** and **rendered view**

- Export notes as `.md` (Markdown), `.pdf`, or `.txt`
- Supports GitHub-Flavored Markdown for developers

The iPad Notes app now becomes a **multi-environment editor** where you can:

- Write blog posts in Markdown
- Take lecture notes and publish them
- Document code projects or APIs
- Plan content with clear headings and bullet points

Writing Experience

Markdown support works seamlessly with:

- **Magic Keyboard** and external keyboards
- **Apple Pencil handwriting-to-text**
- **Voice dictation**, which supports punctuation and headers

For example:

Weekly Agenda

Monday
- Team meeting at 9AM
- Code review

Tuesday
- Write chapter 10
- Edit publishing draft

This appears instantly in rendered form, with headings, bullet points, and spacing.

Collaboration and Version Control

Markdown is favored in team environments, and Notes in iPadOS 26 allows:

- **Real-time collaboration** on Markdown documents

- **Tracked changes** with highlights and suggested edits

- **Version history** so you can roll back edits

- Drag-and-drop capabilities into Markdown-compatible apps like Notion, Ulysses, or Obsidian

This turns Notes into a **lightweight IDE (integrated development environment)** for writing, planning, and prototyping.

Security and Portability

Notes with Markdown can be:

- **Locked with Face ID**

- **Synced via iCloud** across all devices

- **Exported** to Github or shared via AirDrop

- Integrated with **Shortcuts** for automation (e.g., publish blog on WordPress with one tap)

Markdown notes are also searchable and support tags, making it easy to **organize projects** by folder, theme, or topic.

Conclusion

With Markdown integration, the Notes app in iPadOS 26 becomes more than a digital notepad—it becomes a **professional writing platform**. Whether you're building a knowledge base, writing documentation, or planning a book, Markdown adds the simplicity and power users have long been waiting for.

Writing with the Reed Pen in Apple Pencil Apps

The **reed pen tool** introduced in iPadOS 26 elevates digital handwriting and calligraphy by emulating the feel and dynamics of traditional writing instruments. With **stroke-angle presets**, pressure sensitivity, and ink simulation, this tool unlocks a new level of precision and artistry in apps like **Notes, Preview, Freeform, and Journal**.

What is the Reed Pen?

The reed pen is modeled after classical writing tools used in:

- Arabic, Japanese, and Chinese calligraphy
- Manuscript art
- Historical scripts and ornate handwriting

In iPadOS 26, the digital reed pen:

- Responds to angle, speed, and pressure

- Creates broad and thin strokes in real-time

- Offers **customizable nib styles**, ink opacity, and flow

Whether you are signing documents, sketching logos, or practicing penmanship, the reed pen provides **authentic control and fluidity**.

Using the Reed Pen in Notes and Freeform

In **Notes**, the reed pen can be used for:

- Elegant headings

- Annotating documents with flourish

- Signature creation

In **Freeform**, users can:

- Create intricate diagrams

- Design ornate lettering

- Blend colors and pen widths in custom artwork

Every line drawn responds to:

- **Tilt**: simulate natural pen angle
- **Speed**: adjust ink saturation
- **Pressure**: create bold or whisper-thin lines

Document Markup with Style

In **Preview**, users can:

- Sign contracts with signature-quality finesse
- Annotate PDFs in a formal or stylized manner
- Use the pen to underline, circle, or write directly on documents with elegant flair

For professionals, this adds a level of polish and personalization that feels **less robotic and more human**.

Learning and Practicing Calligraphy

Apple has included **practice templates** within Journal and Notes:

- Latin script, cursive, and Japanese characters

- Guides for stroke order, width, and angle

- Auto-correction tools for learning pen control

Combined with **haptic feedback** and **audio cues**, users receive subtle confirmation of good technique, making it a perfect tool for:

- Students learning calligraphy

- Artists developing logos or brand fonts

- Anyone wanting to improve handwriting or self-expression

Cross-App Consistency and Customization

The reed pen experience is consistent across all PencilKit-enabled apps, and users can:

- Save **preset styles**

- Create **custom nibs**

- Use **Shortcuts** to switch pen modes on command

Whether drawing in Procreate or writing in Journal, the reed pen keeps its attributes, giving users a sense of **cohesive tool mastery**.

Conclusion

The **reed pen in iPadOS 26** combines **ancient artistry with modern technology**. It's not just a new drawing tool—it's a gateway into elegant writing, expressive annotations, and artistic exploration that elevates the iPad's appeal to **creatives, educators, and professionals** alike.

Chapter 11: Accessibility and Inclusivity

Accessibility Reader and Braille Access

iPadOS 26 brings transformative changes in accessibility, continuing Apple's long-standing commitment to empowering users of all abilities. With the introduction of the **Accessibility Reader** and an all-new **Braille Access** experience, Apple reaffirms that every user deserves a seamless, dignified, and fully functional experience on iPad.

Introducing Accessibility Reader

The new **Accessibility Reader** is a **systemwide reading mode** designed to assist users who are blind, have low vision, or have reading difficulties such as **dyslexia** or cognitive impairments. It's an evolution of Speak Screen and Reader View, now fully integrated across apps and dynamic content types.

Key features of Accessibility Reader include:

- **Simplified formatting**: Removes ads, navigation bars, and non-essential UI elements, presenting text in a clean, scrollable layout.

- **Customizable fonts and colors**: Choose from dyslexia-friendly fonts, alter text size, change background color for visual comfort, and increase line spacing.

- **Text-to-Speech (TTS)**: Real-time voice narration with adjustable speaking rate, voice style, and language options.

- **Focus Mode**: Highlights each word or sentence as it's read aloud, aiding users with cognitive or attention disorders.

- **Integration with Apple Pencil**: Users can tap or highlight with Apple Pencil to initiate speech or notes.

- **Offline Access**: Downloads articles or documents to be read aloud without requiring an internet connection — great for on-the-go learners.

Whether you're a student who needs structured content, a senior seeking easier readability, or someone managing neurodivergent needs, **Accessibility Reader** removes barriers and enhances comprehension.

Using Accessibility Reader in iPadOS 26

Once enabled via **Settings > Accessibility > Reading**, Accessibility Reader can be activated:

- With a **two-finger swipe down** from the top of the screen

- By **long-pressing text** and tapping "Speak"

- Or automatically in supported apps like Safari, Mail, Notes, and Books

A discreet **floating toolbar** gives users quick access to pause, rewind, skip sentences, and adjust the visual format on the fly.

The Power of Braille Access

For users with **visual impairments**, Braille remains one of the most effective methods of literacy and information access. iPadOS 26 introduces **Braille Access**, a completely reimagined experience designed for **external Braille displays** and **VoiceOver users**.

Notable enhancements include:

- **Simplified pairing**: iPad automatically recognizes certified Braille displays and connects instantly via Bluetooth.

- **Multi-language support**: Over 40 languages with Grade 1 and Grade 2 Braille support.

- **Cursor routing**: Lets users interact directly with the screen content via tactile feedback.

- **Auto-translation**: Instantly converts text to Braille and vice versa, making communication and document creation seamless.

- **Navigation enhancements**: Use rotor gestures to navigate by headings, links, tables, or even page elements in PDF documents.

The integration is **deep and consistent**, meaning whether you're composing emails, browsing the web, or marking up a PDF, Braille users get **equal access and full functionality**.

Accessibility APIs for Developers

Apple also introduced **new APIs** to allow third-party developers to:

- Provide **Braille output** and control schemes within their own apps

- Automatically adopt **reader view rendering**

- Offer **custom actions** for switch control or assistive touch

- Support for **Live Regions**, ensuring updates are spoken immediately without user navigation

This means that apps like Kindle, Slack, or Microsoft Word can now be just as accessible as Apple-native apps — a massive win for inclusivity.

Conclusion

The **Accessibility Reader** and **Braille Access** in iPadOS 26 aren't just assistive technologies — they're **empowerment tools**. They reflect Apple's vision of a world where no ability is a limitation, and everyone has the right to education, creativity, and connection.

Sharing Accessibility Settings Across Devices

Another breakthrough feature in iPadOS 26 is **Shared Accessibility Profiles** — a feature that enables users to **sync their customized accessibility preferences** across all their Apple devices.

Why It Matters

For users who rely on specific configurations — such as **VoiceOver, Zoom, Magnifier, Color Filters, AssistiveTouch, or Sound Recognition** — having to repeat those settings manually across devices is tedious and inefficient.

Shared Accessibility Settings now enable:

- Instant **sync across iPhone, iPad, and Mac** through iCloud

- Temporary **accessibility profiles for shared devices** (e.g., school iPads or library iMacs)

- Easy **backup and restore** of accessibility settings after device reset or replacement

How to Set It Up

To enable settings synchronization:

1. Go to **Settings > Accessibility > Share Across Devices**

2. Toggle **"Sync Accessibility Settings via iCloud"**

3. Sign in with the **same Apple ID** on other devices

4. Custom settings will begin syncing automatically

For users managing **multiple devices**, such as an iPhone and an iPad, this ensures a seamless experience. You'll find:

- **Zoom** levels matching perfectly
- **VoiceOver gestures** behaving the same across devices
- **Hearing aid pairings** syncing with ease

Temporary Profiles for Shared Use

In educational or caregiving environments, iPadOS 26 allows for **temporary accessibility profiles** via **AirDrop or QR code**. For example:

- A visually impaired student can scan a QR on a classroom iPad and instantly apply their accessibility preferences.
- A caregiver can set up a profile on their iPhone and beam it to a loved one's iPad before they start using it.

Once the session ends, the device returns to its **default state**, ensuring privacy and usability for all.

Practical Use Cases

- **Schools**: Students with disabilities use shared iPads with their exact settings applied per session

- **Rehabilitation centers**: Therapists load patient-specific motor control settings before therapy

- **Libraries and public iPads**: Accessibility can be tailored on-demand, helping users with hearing, vision, or dexterity issues

Conclusion

The ability to **share accessibility settings across devices** transforms Apple's ecosystem into a truly **personalized and portable experience**. It's a game-changer for users with special needs, providing freedom, autonomy, and dignity — regardless of the device they're using.

Customizing iPadOS 26 for Every User

Inclusivity isn't about a one-size-fits-all model — it's about **adapting technology to fit the individual**. iPadOS 26 introduces a refined suite of **customization**

options that allow every user to tailor their iPad experience to their own unique needs, preferences, and challenges.

1. Visual Customizations

For users with low vision, light sensitivity, or cognitive impairments, visual adjustments can dramatically improve usability.

- **Display & Text Size**: Increase contrast, reduce transparency, and apply color filters for easier viewing.

- **Color Inversion and Grayscale**: Helps users with light sensitivity or specific vision conditions.

- **Reduce Motion**: Minimizes parallax and animation effects that can cause dizziness or disorientation.

- **Pointer Style**: Customize the appearance and behavior of the on-screen pointer for external mouse use.

2. Audio and Hearing Accessibility

iPadOS 26 includes support for:

- **Live Listen** with AirPods for enhanced hearing

- **Sound Recognition**: Detects alarms, doorbells, crying, and more

- **Mono Audio**: For users with hearing loss in one ear

- **Hearing Aid Support**: Seamless integration with Made-for-iPhone (MFi) hearing devices

New in iPadOS 26, users can now:

- Assign **custom ringtones for alerts** to differentiate warnings

- Route audio from specific apps to **different outputs**, perfect for multitasking and media balancing

3. Motor and Touch Adjustments

For users with **limited mobility or motor control**, Apple offers tools like:

- **AssistiveTouch**: Use on-screen gestures and menus instead of physical buttons

- **Switch Control**: Navigate iPad using adaptive switches or external devices

- **Touch Accommodations**: Adjust how touch gestures are recognized (e.g., hold duration, swipe delay)

- **Voice Control**: Navigate iPad entirely through spoken commands

4. Cognitive Accessibility

Apple now includes:

- **Guided Access**: Lock iPad into a single app or limit interaction time

- **Focus Filters**: Limit screen time distractions for users with ADHD or similar conditions

- **Accessibility Shortcut**: Triple-click the side button to quickly enable or disable accessibility features

Additionally, **Focus Modes** can now integrate **accessibility triggers**, such as automatically enabling VoiceOver or increasing text size during reading hours.

5. Custom Shortcuts for Accessibility

Users can create **automated routines** using the Shortcuts app:

- "When I open Books, enable Accessibility Reader"

- "When I arrive at school, turn on VoiceOver"

- "When I plug in AirPods, enable Sound Recognition"

This empowers users to build a **fully adaptive iPad experience** that responds intelligently to their lifestyle and needs.

Conclusion

With these deeply integrated tools and settings, iPadOS 26 is no longer just customizable — it's **malleable**, reshaping itself to support users as **individuals**. Whether you're blind, deaf, neurodivergent, or physically impaired, Apple has built an ecosystem that respects, supports, and **adapts to you**.

Chapter 12: Tips, Tricks & Hidden Features

Lesser-Known Features That Will Boost Your Workflow

While iPadOS 26 introduces big, flashy upgrades like Liquid Glass, Apple Intelligence, and the new windowing system, some of its most powerful tools lie beneath the surface. These **lesser-known features** are often overlooked in favor of marquee updates, but they can **supercharge productivity**, streamline everyday tasks, and transform how users interact with their devices.

1. Quick Note Everywhere

Quick Note has evolved from a gesture-based feature into a **fully integrated system** across iPadOS 26. By swiping from the bottom-right corner or tapping with Apple Pencil, users can now invoke **Quick Note anywhere** — in Safari, Mail, Calendar, or even third-party apps.

What's more, Quick Notes now **remember app context**, meaning when you jot something down while browsing a webpage or reading an email, tapping the note later takes you straight back to that specific content.

2. Persistent Clipboard History

iPadOS 26 introduces **Clipboard Stacks** — an unadvertised but powerful new feature that stores your last five clipboard items automatically. With a simple three-finger tap (or through the new **Keyboard Shortcut** ⌘⇧V), users can **cycle through recent copied content** — including images, URLs, and text snippets.

This is invaluable for writers, coders, designers, and multitaskers who copy-paste frequently and hate redoing work.

3. Drag and Drop 2.0

Drag and Drop has been refreshed to work **across all app windows** — even from **floating or tiled windows**. You can drag a photo from Files, text from Safari, or a note from Notes and drop it anywhere in split-screen or Stage Manager without losing context.

Additionally, dragging **multiple items** now works better with **haptic feedback**, showing each added item with a subtle vibration, making multitasking intuitive and tactile.

4. App Shelf Enhancements

The **App Shelf**, first introduced in iPadOS 15, has received subtle improvements. You can now:

- Access **recent app windows** with a long-press on the dock

- Pin specific **app instances** (e.g., a specific Safari tab group or Pages document)

- Close, rename, or organize windows directly from the Shelf without opening them

This turns the Shelf into a **workflow hub** rather than just a window manager.

5. Enhanced Scribble Support

Scribble now recognizes **diagrams, flowcharts, and even math formulas**, allowing Apple Pencil users to draw basic shapes or charts, which iPadOS then **autocorrects and labels**. The experience feels organic, especially in apps like **Freeform** and **Notes**.

Additionally, Scribble now supports **multi-language recognition** — useful for multilingual users or those working in language-learning contexts.

6. Floating Dock for Quick Apps

If you're juggling multiple apps but want something more minimal than Stage Manager, try **Floating Dock Apps**. By dragging an app icon from the dock slightly upward (without committing to a split view), you can create a **floating card** of the app for quick interaction

— perfect for checking messages or calendar events without disrupting your main task.

Power User Tips for Faster Navigation

If you're ready to go from casual iPad user to **power user**, these tips will give you the speed and control of a desktop-level workflow. iPadOS 26 is more than a tablet OS — it's a full productivity platform when you know where to look.

1. Mastering Multitouch Gestures

Beyond the usual swipe up/down, iPadOS 26 now supports **multi-finger directional swipes**, including:

- **Three-finger swipe left/right** to undo/redo

- **Four-finger swipe up** to open Exposé

- **Pinch with three fingers** to **copy**, **spread with three** to **paste**

Combined with the windowing system, these gestures make navigation lightning-fast.

2. Using Keyboard Shortcuts like a Pro

Connect a Magic Keyboard or external keyboard and unlock over **100 new shortcuts**, now listed in **Settings > Keyboard > Shortcuts**.

Some essential ones:

- ⌘H – Return to Home

- ⌘Tab – App Switcher

- ⌘Shift+T – Open Last Closed Tab (Safari)

- ⌘Option+Arrow – Move between window tiles

- ⌘Space – Spotlight Search

With the new **Searchable Shortcut Menu**, you can press and hold ⌘ in any app to view supported commands instantly.

3. Spotlight on Steroids

Spotlight Search is now smarter, allowing you to:

- Search **files within folders**

- Trigger **web shortcuts**

- Launch **shortcuts and automations**

- Search **inside emails, messages, and PDFs**

You can even ask natural-language queries like:

"Find the PDF I downloaded last week with the name 'invoice'"
or
"Search all emails from John with attachments"

This turns Spotlight into your **command center**.

4. App-Specific Widgets and Interactivity

Widgets are no longer just informative — they're **interactive and dynamic**. You can:

- **Reply to messages** from the Messages widget

- **Complete tasks** in Reminders

- **Control smart devices** in Home without launching the app

- Use **third-party widgets** to create mini dashboards

And with **widget stacks**, swipe between multiple widgets in the same spot — curated for your current focus mode or time of day.

137

5. Quick Access with Focus Mode Triggers

Focus Modes in iPadOS 26 go beyond Do Not Disturb. You can now:

- Trigger **app-specific layouts**
- Enable/disable **accessibility settings**
- Automate **Shortcuts** per focus mode
- Change **Home Screen appearance** dynamically

This allows you to create modes like:

- "Writing Focus" — Distraction-free Notes and Grammarly with keyboard
- "Night Focus" — Low brightness, blue light filter, Calm widget
- "Work Focus" — Files + Mail on main screen, Slack notifications enabled

Custom Shortcuts and Automation Ideas

The **Shortcuts app** continues to evolve into the iPad's brain — and now with Apple Intelligence integration, it's smarter, more proactive, and even more visual.

Here's how to make **automation your superpower** in iPadOS 26.

1. Shortcuts + Apple Intelligence

With AI models now available to Shortcuts, you can:

- **Summarize long articles** from Safari into Notes

- **Compare text from a lecture and your notes** to find missing information

- **Convert voice memos into actionable checklists**

These are created using new blocks like:

- "Use Writing Tools to Summarize"

- "Compare Text Sources"

- "Generate Checklist from Voice Input"

2. Contextual Automation Ideas

Create **location-based or time-based shortcuts**, such as:

- **When I arrive at work** → Open Mail, Calendar, Slack
- **At 9 PM** → Turn on Night Focus, open Journal
- **When I connect AirPods** → Launch Music, set volume to 70%

These can all be managed from the new **Shortcut Suggestions screen** based on behavior and usage.

3. Daily Routine Templates

Here are ready-to-use templates for real-life routines:

Morning Routine:

- Read weather aloud
- Show calendar events
- Turn on Smart Lights

140

- Launch Fitness+

Study Mode:

- Activate Do Not Disturb
- Open PDF Textbook
- Start Pomodoro timer
- Log session in Notes

Journal Automation:

- At 8 PM → Ask "What did you learn today?"
- Open Journal with template entry
- Include weather + photo of the day

4. System Control Shortcuts

Control iPadOS like never before:

- Toggle **Dark Mode**
- Switch audio output between apps

- Rotate screen lock on/off

- Clear clipboard history

- Enable/disable VoiceOver or Zoom

These small actions make for big improvements in accessibility and speed.

5. Sharing and Installing Shortcuts

Shortcuts can now be shared **via QR code, iMessage**, or even **AirDrop**. Third-party shortcut libraries like RoutineHub, MacStories, and Reddit r/Shortcuts continue to grow.

Be sure to **audit permissions** when installing — iPadOS 26 will now alert you if a shortcut accesses private data or performs sensitive actions.

■ **Final Thoughts**

The true power of **iPadOS 26** lies not just in its headline features but in the **little things** — the shortcuts, hidden gestures, automations, and tweaks that turn your iPad into a **custom-built productivity machine**. Whether you're a student, a creative pro, a business user, or just someone who loves efficiency, these lesser-known tricks and power-user tips can **save** hours of time, **reduce friction**, and make your iPad feel uniquely yours.

■ Chapter 13: Troubleshooting and FAQs

Common Issues After Updating

Updating to a new operating system can be exciting, but it's also not uncommon for users to experience hiccups during or after the transition. With iPadOS 26 being one of Apple's most significant releases, some issues — both big and small — can arise. This section will walk you through the most **common post-update issues**, explain why they happen, and show you how to resolve them efficiently.

1. Battery Draining Too Fast

Symptom: After updating, your iPad battery seems to run out much quicker than before.

Causes:

- Indexing background files post-update.

- Apps running outdated code not optimized for iPadOS 26.

- New features (like **Apple Intelligence**, Background Tasks, or Location Services) consuming more power.

Solutions:

- Give your iPad 24–48 hours to finish background tasks like re-indexing.

- Go to **Settings > Battery** to see which apps are draining the most power.

- Disable non-essential features: **Settings > Privacy > Location Services** or turn off **Background App Refresh**.

- Consider performing a **force restart**: Press and quickly release the Volume Up button, then the Volume Down button, and finally press and hold the Top button until the Apple logo appears.

---

2. Wi-Fi or Bluetooth Connectivity Problems

Symptom: Dropped Wi-Fi connections or issues pairing with Bluetooth devices.

Causes:

- Reset network settings during the update.

- Bluetooth pairing cache disrupted.

- Changes to permissions or background activity in iPadOS 26.

Solutions:

- Reset Network Settings: **Settings > General > Transfer or Reset iPad > Reset > Reset Network Settings**.

- Forget and re-pair Bluetooth devices: **Settings > Bluetooth > [Device Name] > Forget This Device**.

- Restart router or modem and your iPad.

---

3. App Crashes and Freezing

Symptom: Apps frequently crash or lag after the update.

Causes:

- Apps haven't yet been optimized for iPadOS 26.
- System cache conflicts.
- Incomplete installations during the update.

Solutions:

- Update all apps: **App Store > Tap your Profile > Update All**.
- Reinstall problematic apps.
- Reset iPad Settings (non-destructive): **Settings > General > Transfer or Reset iPad > Reset > Reset All Settings**.

---

4. Apple Pencil Unresponsiveness

Symptom: Your Apple Pencil doesn't pair, or lags significantly.

Causes:

- iPadOS 26 introduces new Apple Pencil APIs that may conflict with older firmware.

- Battery issues with the Apple Pencil.

Solutions:

- Re-pair your Apple Pencil: **Settings > Bluetooth > Forget This Device**, then reconnect.

- Check battery in **Settings > Apple Pencil** or use the widget.

- Charge the Apple Pencil fully for at least 15 minutes and restart the iPad.

---

5. Apple Intelligence or Siri Not Working Properly

Symptom: AI features don't respond or show limited capabilities.

Causes:

- Apple Intelligence only supports M1 or later iPads with specific language settings.

- Siri may be misconfigured post-update.

Solutions:

- Go to **Settings > Siri & Search > Language** and make sure it's set to a supported language (like English – US).

- Ensure you're signed into iCloud with the correct Apple ID and have **Apple Intelligence** enabled under **Settings > Apple Intelligence**.

Managing Storage and Performance

One of the most frequent user concerns with a major OS update is **device slowdown or insufficient storage space**. Fortunately, iPadOS 26 provides both tools and strategies to keep your device running smoothly, even under heavy workloads.

1. Understanding System Storage Usage

After updating to iPadOS 26, many users find that their **System Data** has ballooned. This is often due to:

- Caches from Safari or third-party apps.

- Logs from Background Tasks or diagnostics.

- Temporary files from the update itself.

To manage it:

- Go to **Settings > General > iPad Storage** and review space used.

- Offload large apps you don't use often.

- Tap into each app to clear cache (if available) or delete unused documents and data.

---

2. Clearing App Cache and Temporary Files

iPadOS 26 allows for more app control under Settings:

- In **Safari > Advanced > Website Data**, tap **Remove All Website Data**.

- In apps like Files, delete old PDFs, videos, or downloads.

- Third-party file managers and cleanup tools are also available via the App Store, but choose reputable ones only.

3. Optimizing Background Activity

New features like Background Tasks in iPadOS 26 are powerful, but they can also consume RAM and processing power.

To manage:

- Navigate to **Settings > General > Background App Refresh**, and disable apps that don't need constant updating.

- Disable location-based suggestions and notifications via **Settings > Privacy & Security > Location Services**.

4. Use Focus Modes to Save Power and Performance

Activating a **custom Focus Mode** can help restrict apps and background services:

- Create a "Low Power Focus" with minimal notifications and background tasks.

- Disable animations by enabling **Reduce Motion** in **Settings > Accessibility**.

5. Using iCloud and External Drives

Don't let local storage hold you back. Offload data using:

- **iCloud Drive**: Enable **Optimize iPad Storage** under **Settings > Apple ID > iCloud > Photos/Files**.

- **External Drives**: Connect USB-C or Lightning drives using the **Files app**, which now supports folder tagging, batch move, and file previews.

Resetting, Restoring, and Recovery Mode

Even with all the precautions and optimizations, sometimes you'll need to **reset**, **restore**, or put your iPad into **recovery mode**. These are powerful tools to get your device working again if things go wrong.

1. Reset Options Explained

In iPadOS 26, you can find resets under:
Settings > General > Transfer or Reset iPad > Reset, where you'll see:

- **Reset All Settings**: Keeps data but resets preferences (safe and effective for most issues).

- **Erase All Content and Settings**: Full reset — removes apps, data, and settings. Ideal before selling or troubleshooting persistent bugs.

- **Reset Network Settings**: Fixes Wi-Fi, Bluetooth, and VPN issues.

- **Reset Keyboard Dictionary**, **Home Screen Layout**, or **Location & Privacy** — great for niche problems.

---

2. Restoring from iCloud or Mac

If a reset didn't work, **restore from backup**:

- On iPad: During setup after erase, choose **Restore from iCloud Backup**.

- On Mac: Connect iPad > Finder > Select your iPad > Click **Restore Backup**.

Make sure the backup was made using iPadOS 26 or later for best compatibility.

3. Entering Recovery Mode

Use **Recovery Mode** if:

- The device is stuck on the Apple logo.
- It freezes during the update.
- You forgot your passcode.

Steps:

1. Connect iPad to Mac/PC.
2. Press and quickly release the **Volume Up** button.
3. Press and quickly release the **Volume Down** button.
4. Hold the **Top button** until you see the recovery screen (cable pointing to computer).
5. On Mac/PC, choose **Update** (non-destructive) or **Restore** (erases everything).

---

4. Using DFU Mode (Advanced)

DFU (Device Firmware Update) Mode is a deeper reset option:

- Used when Recovery Mode fails.

- Requires iTunes or Finder.

- Completely wipes the device and reinstalls firmware.

Note: Use only as a last resort. Consult Apple Support before proceeding.

---

5. When to Visit an Apple Store

If you experience:

- Hardware-related battery issues.

- Display flickering or unresponsive touch.

- Persistent crashes even after restore.

It's time to consult **Apple Support** or visit a **Genius Bar**. Make sure to:

- Back up data.

- Bring proof of purchase (for warranty status).

- Know your Apple ID and password.

■ Final Tips

- Always keep a **Time Machine–style habit** of backing up your iPad weekly.

- Install updates promptly, especially security patches.

- Monitor Apple's forums and support page for known bugs and fixes.

With the right approach, troubleshooting iPadOS 26 is not only manageable but empowering. Your iPad is built to be resilient — and with these tools, so are you.

■ Appendix

Supported Devices and Feature Availability

With iPadOS 26, Apple continues its trend of refining software experiences for users across a wide variety of iPad models. However, as the system becomes more sophisticated—especially with the introduction of **Apple Intelligence**, advanced windowing, and enhanced creative tools—not all features are available on every device. In this section, we'll take a detailed look at **which iPads support iPadOS 26**, the **hardware requirements for individual features**, and what users can expect in terms of **performance and availability** across the board.

iPad Models Compatible with iPadOS 26

The following devices are officially supported and eligible to receive the iPadOS 26 update:

- **iPad Pro (M4)**

- iPad Pro 12.9-inch (3rd generation and later)

- iPad Pro 11-inch (1st generation and later)

- iPad Air (M2 and later)

- iPad Air (3rd generation and later)

- iPad (A16-based)

- iPad (8th generation and later)

- iPad mini (A17 Pro)

- iPad mini (5th generation and later)

While all of these devices are eligible for the core iPadOS 26 experience, certain features—particularly those reliant on high-performance computing or Apple Intelligence—require newer chips and more memory.

Apple Intelligence: M-Series and A17 Pro Only

One of the most anticipated features in iPadOS 26 is **Apple Intelligence**. Unfortunately, this capability is restricted to specific devices due to its reliance on the

Neural Engine, advanced GPUs, and RAM bandwidth. Devices that fully support Apple Intelligence include:

- **iPad Pro (M4 and M2)**
- **iPad Air (M2)**
- **iPad mini (A17 Pro)**

This means if you're using an A14 or A15-based iPad, while you'll still receive the update and many benefits like the new windowing system and Files improvements, you won't get Apple Intelligence features such as **Live Translation**, **Image Playground**, **Genmoji**, and **Smart Shortcuts**.

Feature Availability Matrix

Feature	Supported Models
Liquid Glass Interface	All supported devices
Windowing System	All supported devices
Stage Manager with External Display	M1 iPads and later
Apple Intelligence	M1 and later, A17 Pro

Genmoji & Image Playground	M1 and later, A17 Pro
Background Tasks API	All devices, but performance may vary
New Files app features	All supported devices
Local Capture for Audio/Video	M1 and newer only
FaceTime Live Translation	Apple Intelligence devices
Math Notes in Calculator	All supported devices
Preview App	All supported devices

Performance Tips for Older Devices

While older iPads can run iPadOS 26, performance may be slightly impacted depending on your device's processor, storage, and usage habits.

Tips:

- Limit multitasking to 2 apps at a time.

- Disable Background App Refresh to conserve memory.

- Avoid installing large apps if storage is under 10GB.

- Reset device settings occasionally to free up resources.

If you're using an older iPad but still want a modern experience, consider investing in external accessories such as a **keyboard case**, **Apple Pencil (1st or 2nd Gen)**, or **USB-C drives** that work seamlessly with iPadOS 26.

Apple Intelligence Language Support Timeline

Apple Intelligence is one of the biggest AI rollouts ever integrated into iPadOS. It powers translation, smart interactions, context-aware recommendations, and more. But since language support is crucial for AI to function effectively, Apple has opted for a **staggered rollout of languages**.

In this section, we'll explore:

- Which languages are supported today.

- What's on the roadmap.

- How to check your iPad's language and Siri settings to ensure compatibility.

Languages Supported at Launch

To ensure optimal accuracy and efficiency, Apple is focusing first on widely-used global languages, especially those with robust datasets. As of the launch of iPadOS 26, **Apple Intelligence supports** the following languages:

- **English (U.S., UK, Canada, Australia)**

- **Spanish (Latin America, Spain)**

- **French**

- **German**

- **Italian**

- **Portuguese (Brazilian)**

- **Japanese**

- **Korean**

- **Chinese (Simplified)**

To use Apple Intelligence, your device must:

- Be on iPadOS 26.

- Be one of the supported models (M1 or A17 Pro).

- Have **Siri and device language set to the same supported language.**

You can adjust this under **Settings > General > Language & Region** and **Settings > Siri & Search > Language**.

Languages Coming by End of 2025

Apple has officially announced a second wave of languages expected by the end of 2025, including:

- **Danish**

- **Dutch**

- **Norwegian**

- **Portuguese (Portugal)**
- **Swedish**
- **Turkish**
- **Chinese (Traditional)**
- **Vietnamese**

This list may expand, especially as Apple collects more data and user feedback. iPads set to these languages may still receive limited Apple Intelligence interactions initially, but full support will roll out progressively.

How to Know If a Feature Is Supported

The best way to know if your preferred language supports a feature:

1. Go to **Settings > Apple Intelligence**.

2. If your device supports it, you'll see toggles for **Live Translation**, **Smart Shortcuts**, and **Image Playground**.

3. If you see a message like "Apple Intelligence is not supported in your language," try changing

Siri and system language temporarily to English to access and test features.

Additional Resources and Apple Support

Even with the best guide at your fingertips, sometimes you need a bit more help—whether it's solving a niche technical issue or exploring a hidden feature Apple quietly introduced. Here's your comprehensive list of **official resources**, **community help**, and **recommended tools** to get the most out of iPadOS 26.

1. Apple's Official Help Resources

Apple provides numerous channels for education and support:

- **Apple Support App**
  Download it from the App Store. It connects you with support agents, Genius Bar appointments, and step-by-step troubleshooting guides.

- **support.apple.com/ipad**
  The home for iPad documentation. Topics

include setup, security, parental controls, iCloud syncing, and more.

- **Apple Community Forums**
  Accessible via discussions.apple.com. Engage with millions of Apple users and troubleshoot unique issues.

- **Apple Developer Site**
  For advanced users and developers. Visit developer.apple.com/ipados for documentation, API changes, and developer beta releases.

2. YouTube and Third-Party Tutorials

If you prefer visual guidance, check out:

- **iJustine, Marques Brownlee (MKBHD),** and **Rene Ritchie** on YouTube.

- Udemy and Skillshare courses focused on iPad productivity.

- Blogs like **9to5Mac, MacRumors,** and **iMore** often feature walkthroughs and reviews of new features.

3. Third-Party Tools and Apps

These tools can extend your iPadOS 26 experience:

- **Readdle's Documents** – More advanced file management.

- **GoodNotes 6** – Incredible Apple Pencil support for note-taking.

- **LumaFusion** – Professional video editing.

- **Shortcuts Gallery** – Download and import prebuilt Shortcuts.

Make sure your apps are regularly updated to support iPadOS 26 APIs and performance standards.

4. Accessibility Support

If you or someone you support relies on **VoiceOver**, **Braille displays**, or **custom hearing or vision settings**, Apple offers specialized resources:

- **Accessibility Support Line:** Call toll-free (U.S. and select countries).

- **Accessibility Portal:** apple.com/accessibility – Full overview of vision, hearing, mobility, and cognitive tools.

You can also join the **AppleSeed for IT program** to preview accessibility features and provide feedback directly to Apple.

---

5. Feedback and Reporting Bugs

Found a bug? Want to request a feature?

- Use the **Feedback Assistant** app (pre-installed on beta versions or available via TestFlight).

- Tap **Settings > Privacy & Security > Analytics & Improvements** to allow anonymous diagnostics.

- Visit **feedbackassistant.apple.com** to log in with your Apple ID and submit detailed bug reports.

Apple regularly updates iPadOS based on feedback from public beta testers and support ticket trends. Your input shapes the future of the platform.

Printed in Dunstable, United Kingdom